VOICES FROM THE PAST

Copyright © 2014 by Hairenik Press

All rights reserved. This book or any portion thereof may not be reproduced or used in any manner whatsoever without the express written permission of the publisher except for the use of brief quotations in a book review.

Printed in the United States of America

ISBN 978-1-940573-07-6
LCCN 2014904971

Hairenik
80 Bigelow Avenue
Watertown, MA 02472
www.Hairenik.com

VOICES FROM THE PAST
EXCERPTS FROM THE WRITINGS OF
ARMENIAN REVOLUTIONARIES

EDITED AND TRANSLATED BY VAHE HABESHIAN

CONTENTS

Introduction vii
Kristapor Mikayelian 1
Stepan Zorian (Rostom) 5
Simon Zavarian 9
Khanasora Vardan (Sargis Mehrabian) 13
Hovhannes Yousoufian (Melik T. Vahanian) 17
Haroutiun Shahrigian (Nitra, Adom) 21
Hovnan Davtian (Honan Nanoyian) 25
Avetis Aharonian 29
General Antranig (Antranig Ozanian) 33
Garegin Khazhak (Chakalian) 37
Nikol Douman (Nikoghayos Ter Hovhannisian) 41
Levon Shant (Levon Seghposian) 45
Yeprem Khan (Davtian) 49
Armen Garo (Garegin Pastermajian) 53
Liparit Nazariants 59
Mariam Makarian (Maro) 63
Mikayel Varandian (Hovhannisian) 67
Sebouh (Arshag Nersesian) 71

Hamo Ohanjanian (Mherian) 75

Papken Siuni (Bedros Parian) 79

Aleksandr Khatisian. 83

Abraham Giulkhandanian 87

Nikol Aghbalian 91

Vahan Papazian (Koms). 95

Siamanto (Adom Yarjanian) 99

Aram Manoukian (Sargis Hovhannisian, Sergey) 103

Rouben Ter Minasian (Minas Ter Minasian) 107

Simon Vratsian (Simon Grouzinian). 113

Reuben Darbinian (Artashes Chilingirian) 117

Vahan Cardashian 121

Dro (Drastamat Kanayan) 125

Schavarch Missakian (Shavarsh Misakian) 129

Garegin Nzhdeh (Garegin Ter Haroutiunian) 133

Vahan Navasardian 139

Garo Sassouni. 143

Soghomon Tehlirian. 147

Arshavir Shiragian 153

INTRODUCTION

HEEDING THE VOICE OF THE PAST

The origins of this book lie in the "Voices From the Past" columns that regularly appeared in the *Armenian Weekly* for roughly 15 months, from the fall of 1990 to the winter of 1991. That period coincided with the handover of the reins of the *Armenian Weekly* from Antranig Kasbarian to me, the *Weekly*'s assistant editor since 1988.

Each week, I would translate a passage from the writings of a well-known figure of the Armenian liberation movement of the late 19th–early 20th century; I would also compile and translate a biographical sketch and, along with a picture of the featured person, publish all three as that week's column.

To be honest, I don't recall what, exactly, prompted the launch of "Voices From the Past." What I do recall is the atmosphere of the times—the movement for Karabagh's liberation and the independence of Armenia, which framed our daily work at the *Weekly*.

Along with the battles raging on the ground against Soviet and Azerbaijani forces, a war of ideas was also being fought among the political forces and factions in Armenia and the Diaspora. Approaches and beliefs diverged regarding geostrategic orientation, the superiority of one or another political and economic system, the tactical forms that protest and struggle should take…

Frequently, those engaging in that clash of ideas lacked historical insight, whereas they (and the popular movement in Armenia) might have benefited from the lessons of the Armenian revolutionary movement of a century earlier—so similar to the current events of the late '80s and early '90s (and, for that matter, to today's). Meanwhile, others attempted to co-opt symbols of our common past that still resonated in the popular imagination.

I distinctly recall, for example, a wall calendar published and distributed in Armenia by a prominent group that vehemently opposed the ARF; we had received a copy of it at the Hairenik Building. The calendar displayed images of fedayis, with descriptions of the fedayi or the group of fedayis featured each month. Although the vast majority (some 10 of the 12) images were of Dashnaktsakan fighters, nowhere in the calendar was the ARF mentioned.

In any event, whatever the proximate cause of its launch, the "Voices From the Past" column was an attempt to transmit institutional and historical knowledge and insight.

Not surprisingly, then, the arch of Armenian history from the 1890s to the 1940s is reflected in the biographies and writings of the figures presented here, whether rank-and-file fedayi, intellectual, military commander, or statesman. So, too, are the ideas, ideologies, worldviews, and hard-won life-lessons that energized and guided not only the lives of individual Dashnaktsakans but also the collective outlook of Dashnaktsoutiun.

That said, by no means is this a definitive, comprehensive work. On the contrary, it is a mere sampling of the hundreds and thousands of personalities and their works that could potentially have been included. And the circumstances under which those samples were collected were anything but ideal: tight deadlines, limited staff, hard-to-find texts... not to mention the relentless responsibility of having to fill up the remaining 95% of the space in each issue of the newspaper.

So, by necessity, we often took the path of least resistance, publishing materials we could easily find and quickly translate.

Not surprisingly, then, many of the biographies here needed updating before they could be included in this book. The primary source for those updates was the two-volume *Armenian Revolutionary Federation Centennial Album-Atlas,* edited by Hagop Manjikian and published in Los Angeles on the occasion of the 100th Anniversary of the ARF's founding. Also of some (limited) use has been that handiest of timesavers for many a high school and college student: Wikipedia.

Admittedly, many of the translated writings ought to have been revisited as well. But doing so would have called for much longer, more sustained effort than I could manage. We are, therefore, left with the translations from some 23 years ago, with only minor edits made to patch up some imperfections.

TRANSLITERATION

Finally, for the curious, a word about transliteration: The task of rendering Armenian words in Latin characters would likely have been easiest if I'd used the approach taken by scholars—that is, using Classical/Eastern Armenian pronunciation as the basis of transliteration. The method used here, though, is a hybrid: Using Western Armenian pronunciation if the person in question was a speaker of Western Armenian or was born in Western Armenia ("Antranig"

| ix

rather than "Andranik," for example), and Eastern Armenian pronunciation in the case of Eastern Armenians. That approach applies to their names as well as the titles of their written works. However, in the case of place names and other proper nouns ("Dashnaktsoutiun," for example, and the names of newspapers), almost always the Eastern Armenian pronunciation has been used.

ACKNOWLEDGMENTS

Aram Hovagimian has been the prime mover behind the publication of this book, efficiently project-managing every imaginable aspect of it on behalf of the ARF Central Committee. Thanks, Aram, for tolerating my procrastinations.

Much thanks, also, to Khatchig Mouradian and Nanore Barsoumian, editor and assistant editor, respectively, of the *Armenian Weekly*, who sifted through past issues of the *Weekly* to compile the "Voices From the Past" columns. The unenviable task of scanning and digitizing those columns fell to Valerie Johnson of the AYF. Many thanks to Valerie for her thorough work. Much appreciation, too, to Zaven Torikian of the *Hairenik* and the rest of the staff for their assistance, and to Hovsep Avakian, for helping to coordinate local events for the launch of this book. A nod of gratitude, as well, to Antranig Kasbarian for reviewing the final text and making valuable suggestions.

Finally, but foremost, I thank Tatul Sonentz-Papazian, former editor of the *Armenian Review*, former director of the ARF and First Republic of Armenia Archives, in Watertown, MA, and current head of the publications department of the Armenian Relief Society. The living embodiment of institutional (ARF and Hairenik) knowledge and insight, Unger Tatul has been, for decades, a mentor to successive editors at the *Armenian Weekly*. Thanks, Tat, for your wisdom, kindness, and generous friendship over the years.

Vahe Habeshian

KRISTAPOR MIKAYELIAN
1859–1905

BORN IN THE village of Verin Agoulis, in the Goghtn region, southern Nakhijevan, Kristapor Mikayelian graduated from the Normal School (teacher's school) in Tiflis (Tbilisi). He then attended Moscow Agricultural Institute, where he met Simon Zavarian and became involved in Russian revolutionary groups.

Interrupting his studies, in 1887, he returned to Tiflis, where he began an active campaign of organizing and training laborers and Western Armenian immigrants. He taught them to read and write, he instructed them in the use of arms, also imparting revolutionary ideology.

In Tiflis, he established the Yeritasard Hayastan (Young Armenia) organization in an effort to provide support to and unite various Armenian activist groups.

Kristapor became the prime mover in the unification of Armenian revolutionary groups into a "Federation of Armenian Revolutionaries" in 1890. It soon thereafter coalesced into an organization in and of itself: Armenian Revolutionary Federation (Hay Heghapokhakan Dashnaktsoutiun). He was to remain a member of its Bureau, the highest executive body, for the remainder of his life.

Accused of being a revolutionary, Kristapor was arrested in spring 1891 by the Russian authorities and exiled to Bessarabia (now in Moldova and Ukraine), where, with Simon Zavarian, who was also in exile, he published the first issues of *Droshak* (Banner, or Flag), which was to become the central organ of the party.

For the next several years he operated in the Transcaucasus, eventually moving to Galatz (Galati), Romania, where he published the third issue of the Droshak newspaper. He served as its editor for many years, based in Geneva from 1898 onward, and also directed the political relations and propaganda efforts of the party. He also published the bi-monthly *Pro Armenia* with the cooperation of the French intellectual and political elite.

Kristapor conceived and headed the Potorik (Tempest) operation to raise funds for the party from wealthy Armenians, if necessary through coercive methods.

In 1904, Kristapor assumed leadership of the ARF's plot to assassinate the "Bloody Sultan," Abdul Hamid II. He was killed in

1905, the victim of an explosion while testing handheld bombs on Mt. Vitosh (Vitosha), near Sofia, Bulgaria. He was 46 years old.

Until his death, Kristapor remained the central figure of the Dashnaktsoutiun.

*

If in order to justify their indifference people say, "What can I do?" when they have never tried to find out what, in general, there is to do or they have ignored the advice that sought to remind them of their most elementary of responsibilities…

If people try to explain their position toward you by saying that they are "unfamiliar with your work," when they have taken no step whatsoever, and wish to take no steps, to familiarize themselves with that work…

When some oppose you, maintaining that they do not consider "your actions appropriate for reaching the objective," when they in fact have no idea of the method of your struggle and often have no way of knowing, because first, through time your tactics change, and second, it must remain an internal, classified matter…

If some people would have you believe that they "profess other convictions," when in fact they do nothing in accordance with any convictions, or in the name of "supreme interests" they only poison public opinion or day and night fill the air with talk in the name of the "surplus labor" of the workers, but when faced with the "surplus blood" of an entire people they remain cold-hearted stoics; if men, with foolishness characteristic of madmen, continuously reject the clear merits of others when they themselves, with the most daring impudence, demand unconditional respect for their conspicuous shortcomings, their charlatanism, and their arrogant, egotistic mindset...

Then, forgive us, for in any of those cases, we cannot consider ourselves as dealing with an opposition worthy of notice.

From "Patmakan Charik" (Historical Evils), Droshak, No. 3, 1901

STEPAN ZORIAN (ROSTOM)
1867–1919

BORN IN THE village of Tsghna, in Goghtn, Nakhijevan, Rostom completed his secondary education in Tiflis, Georgia. In 1889, he enrolled in the Moscow Institute of Agronomy but was eventually expelled for being a revolutionary. He became a founding member of the Armenian Revolutionary Federation, and from 1891 onward, first in Tiflis then in Tavriz (Tabriz), Persia (Iran), Rostom became one of the most active figures of the Dashnaktsoutiun.

He was present at the First World Congress of the ARF, and

with the input of Kristapor Mikayelian and Simon Zavarian he wrote the introduction (on Ideology) of the ARF's Constitution. He then went to Geneva, where until 1895 he worked on *Droshak,* the ARF's central organ.

In 1895, disguised as a samovar salesman, Rostom was in Karin/Garin (Erzurum), where established revolutionary student associations. He was later sent to Iran and the Caucasus on organizational missions. He subsequently returned to Geneva, remaining there until the Second World Congress of the ARF.

From 1898 onward he settled in Philippopolis (Plovdiv), Bulgaria, where he and his wife, Lisa Melik-Shahnazarian, established an Armenian school. While there, he became the architect of collaboration between the ARF and Macedonian revolutionaries.

Rostom returned to the Caucasus in 1902 and played a leading role in anti-Tsarist activities from 1903 to 1904, and in the Armeno-Tatar (Azeri) conflict of 1905–1906, defending Armenians throughout the Transcaucasus from Tatar atrocities.

He went to Persia to establish cooperation with Persian revolutionaries, assisting Iranian constitutional forces in their uprising against the Shah (1905–1907).

In 1907, the presence of Rostom at the Fourth World Congress was a decisive factor in the synthesis of left- and right-wing tendencies in the ARF.

After attending various congresses of the Socialist International, Rostom returned to Garin and remained there until the Eighth World Congress (1914). In 1915, he played a leading role in organizing the Armenian Volunteer Movement and the formation of the volunteer regiments attached to the Russian army.

In 1918, Rostom was the central figure in the heroic defense of Baku against Ottoman Turkish forces that were attempting to occupy the oil-rich city.

He contracted either typhus or typhoid fever, and died in Tiflis in January 1919, at the age of 52, without having stepped foot in the newly independent Armenian republic.

Rostom's thought leadership, implacable will, and relentless organizational activity left an indelible mark on the ARF and its mode of operation.

*

Each time that thanks to the selfless, constant, and unwavering activities of the revolutionary minority the revolutionary organization gains strength and influence, creates faith in the success of the work, and to a certain degree clears the way for the revolution—each time a commotion arises in the various segments of society. Along with the rising of the revolutionary spirit in the people, all sorts of opportunists, exploiters, usurers, snitches, even traitors—in a word, all manner of snakes that know how to amazingly adapt to conditions and profit from them—come to the fore as "revolutionaries" or sympathizers of the revolution.

Such people are insidious, especially at those moments when with overblown statements and pharisaic gestures they exploit the naiveté and ignorance of the masses. And they are unbearable, they are an affliction and a calamity for the revolutionary movement, when the revolution is confronted with a temporary setback and conditions become difficult for revolutionary workers. During such times, those abhorrent creatures quietly return to their lairs, and in an attempt to conceal their true colors, under the masks of "common sense," "farsightedness," and "love of the people," they continue to toy with the people. Continuing to bear the titles of "revolutionary" or "patriot," they become the most damaging obstacles to real revolutionary work. They are like garbage in large and small piles with various smells and colors strewn along the revolutionary path, polluting the environment.

Every revolutionary worker is compelled from time to time to leave his main work and concern himself with that garbage that falls in his path and impedes his progress. Willingly or unwillingly, from time to time he must take upon himself that repulsive task, despite knowing full well that with the first swing of broom those piles will be exposed, filling the air with their stench. Through that atmosphere of gossip, accusation, and intrigue the true revolutionary must continue toward his main purpose.

From "Vnasakar Tarrer" (Harmful Elements), Droshak, *May 1, 1896*

SIMON ZAVARIAN
1866–1913

BORN IN THE village of Aygehat, in Lori, Armenia, Simon Zavarian completed his secondary schooling in Tiflis and continued his education at the Moscow Agricultural Institute, from which he graduated in 1899. He returned to Tiflis, where he worked closely with Kristapor Mikayelian to establish the Federation of Armenian Revolutionaries in 1890.

He went to Trebizond in October of the same year to assume the post of school principal. He was soon arrested as a revolutionary and returned to the Caucasus, then exiled to Bessarabia by the Russian authorities.

He returned in 1892 and took part in the First World Congress of the ARF, fervently upholding the principle of organizational decentralization. Zavarian drafted the bylaws of the Party with Kristapor and Rostom, and remained a member of the ARF Bureau until his death.

He remained in the Caucasus as a member and the secretary of the ARF Bureau until 1902, when he left for Geneva. There, in the absence of Kristapor, Zavarian coordinated the operations of the Western Bureau of the ARF. He was elected a member of the ARF Responsible Body of Cilicia at the Third World Congress (1904).

Traveling extensively while serving as a state agronomist, he was able to take advantage of his position to conduct research for the ARF. He toured the region of Cilicia with Vardan of Khanasor, and later visited Trebizond, Romania, Geneva, Cyprus, Lebanon, Syria, and Egypt on organizing missions. In 1905, he founded an ARF Student Organization in Beirut. At the Fourth World Congress (1907), he submitted a detailed report on the situation of Armenians in Cilicia and the possibilities for insurrection in the region.

After the Ottoman Constitution was proclaimed in 1908, Zavarian spent two years in Moush and Sasoun, where he held various teaching positions.

He took part in the Fifth (1909) and Sixth (1911) World Congresses of the ARF and settled in Constantinople in the summer of 1911. A member of the Western Bureau, he again taught and also contributed to *Azatamart* (Battle for Liberation), the official newspaper of the ARF in Constantinople from 1908 to 1915.

Zavarian died suddenly in Constantinople of what is thought to have been a heart attack, while on his way to the *Azatamart* publishing house. He was 47 years old.

He was given a national funeral unprecedented in scope, with thousands in attendance. His body was taken to Tiflis to be buried.

Zavarian is considered the personification of the revolutionary and moral consciousness of the Dashnaktsoutiun.

*

All persons are our concern: the broad segments of the people, the masses that live by the fruit of their own labor, those deprived and oppressed classes that have always sustained society, those segments that have constituted the foundation of society and mankind's creativity. They have been deprived of all rights, when, in essence, they are the ones who should be foremost endowed with such rights…

The progress toward perfection—within the bounds of nature—of all men, of all individuals, without class or national distinction, can take place only by creating conditions equally beneficial to all.

The perfection of individual human beings thus expands beyond the realm of the individual and becomes connected to the perfection (re-formation) of public organizations… And because the interrelations and compositions of public organizations historically vary among the nationalities of different countries, that re-formation, too, greatly varies and has differing characteristics.

The Dashnaktsoutiun, conducting its activities in places where

Armenians live—Turkey, Russia, Persia—takes into consideration the conditions of those places. Moreover, having been born of the limitless suffering of the Armenian people, to this day the Dashnaktsoutiun bears its Armenian stamp, even with its purpose being the defense of all the rights—human, national, economic—of the Armenian and neighboring working masses.

Liberation from all sorts of persecution and oppression that constrain the development of the individual—that is the essential consideration for each Dashnaktsakan [ARF member]....

Because the persecution and oppression are multifaceted and occur so often, the struggle must be organized and well thought out. Not only must the most essential and fundamental of the methods of oppression be defined but also, and even more so, the methods of achieving change that are timely and possible to implement.

While evaluating all of that, one must consider not only the conditions of our own environment but also the experiences of other nations. The Ideal created by mankind regarding justice, truth, and progress remains to this day the bright star that guides us... without diverting us from our own [national] environment, without making us forget our true character.

From "Inch En Uzum Dashnaktsakannere" (What do the Dashnaks want?), unpublished

KHANASORA VARDAN (SARGIS MEHRABIAN)
1870?–1943

B ORN IN KARABAGH, Khanasora Vardan (Vardan of Khanasor) gained military experience by serving in the Russian Army. He was the first revolutionary organizer of the Armenians in the Taurus region, south of Lake Van.

From 1890 onward he was in Iran (in Iranian Azerbaijan), in Tabriz, Salmast, and the Derik Monastery, participating in the battles at Derik.

At the head of small groups of fedayis, he often crossed the

Iranian-Turkish border toward Vaspourakan (Van) to transport arms, often engaging in skirmishes with Turkish border guards and Kurdish tribes.

In the spring of 1896, he organized and led the defense of Shatakh, a mountainous region of Vaspourakan. Then, in September of the same year, he took part in the *Bsdik Tebk* (small battles) of Van.

In July 1897 he served as commander-in-chief of the Khanasor punitive expedition against the Mazrik Kurdish tribe, which had earlier massacred hundreds of unarmed Armenian fighters who were evacuating Van, after self-defense battles there, as part of an agreement with the authorities.

Later, he worked alongside Simon Zavarian to assess and organize the Cilician region, as well as Izmir.

During Armeno-Tatar (Azeri) fighting in the Caucasus in 1905–1906, Vardan was placed in charge of the self-defense of Karabagh.

In 1915, he was appointed commander-in-chief of the Araratian Regiment of the Armenian Volunteers, and hastened to assist the Armenian self-defense of Van.

After the Sovietization of the Armenian Republic, Vardan remained. He died in Yerevan, in 1943.

*

We noticed through our binoculars that a large number of people were running away, climbing toward the summits of the mountains. Who were they, and why were they fleeing? Soon it was evident that they were Armenian peasants who had escaped from the villages, and seeing the glistening of our weapons, and thinking us to be Kurds, they were trying to save themselves. A helpless mob with the mentality of sheep who know only to flee and don't think for a moment about countering the force of the enemy with force…. When we came close, a gut-wrenching scene greeted us: women, children, old people, young men, brides and girls, in rags… crying and sobbing, running toward us to come under the protection of our weapons, their salvation…

And for what? [Because] eight Kurds, largely unarmed, had attacked the village; they had killed seven Armenians, looted the village, and left. None of the Armenians had attempted to defend themselves; all had left the village and escaped toward the mountains. The population of three other villages had followed them. No one had been left in the villages; they had even brought the cattle and sheep with them.

What could one do? Pity them? Or spit on the faces of their men? Sometimes a person thinks, Are these people worth sacrificing our lives for? But then we would say to ourselves, They are men like us, is it their fault that centuries of subjugation have resulted in this condition? It is our obligation to save them; the object of the revolution is to make slaves into men…

From Vardan's Memoirs, ca. 1896

HOVHANNES YOUSOUFIAN
(MELIK T. VAHANIAN)
1850–1920

Born in Yerevan to a family from Nor Bayazit, Yousoufian (Vahanian) graduated from the Nersisian College of Tiflis. While a teacher in Telav (Telavi), in eastern Georgia, he was actively involved in revolutionary groups.

Yousoufian became one of the most active and effective organizers during the first decade of the ARF. Under orders from the ARF Bureau, he traveled to Trebizond, Constantinople, Geneva, and the United States, where he established ARF units.

He was a teacher in Trebizond from 1890 to 1892. As the plenipotentiary representative of the ARF in Constantinople from 1893 to 1895, Yousoufian set up a powerful ARF clandestine organization in the capital of the Ottoman Empire.

He was then sent to the United States, where he established the foundation of the US ARF organization (1896–1898).

The ARF's Second World Congress (1898) elected him a member of the Eastern Bureau, but his failing health prevented him from being as active as he once had been.

He was elected Mayor of Nor Bayazit in 1905. He remained in the Caucasus until 1910.

Fleeing Tsarist persecution, he settled in Switzerland, spending the rest of his days, ill and often penniless, in Lausanne,. He died there at the age of 70.

*

Ardashes was a native Bolsetsi and a noted spy and snitch for the police. The spy Ardashes's main arena of operations was the class of the poor, the artisans, the peasants.... And the naive expatriates from [Western] Armenia, taken by the disgusting spy's sweet and syrupy language, opened up to him, told him secrets, made revelations—and the next day or a few days later they were led off to jail, to repent for their sins in dark, dank cells, without knowing that the one who had betrayed them and had them arrested was their friend Ardashes. And even if they had a slight doubt, that too would be dissipated when that brood of hell visited the jail, provided consolation, expressed false condolences.

The spy Ardashes sometimes turned into a raging revolutionary in front of his prey. With false inspiration, and a swaggering unique to Bolsetsis, he spouted hellfire against Turkish oppression, eloquently denounced its evils, often representing himself as a victim of the exploitation. He shed crocodile tears for his wretched brethren, and saying there would no assistance from heaven, he would point to revolution as the means that would grant freedom to all.... He would then give a copy of a revolutionary publication to his interlocutor, begging that he pass it on to others so that the sacred task could progress more quickly. And, a few days later, the jails would again be filled with numerous victims whose only crime was gullibility....

The base activities of the spy were presented in detail to the ARF Central Committee of Constantinople, which in one of its March [1895] meetings... condemned the spy Ardashes to death and gave the responsibility of carrying out that verdict to one of the groups, the terrorists... working under its jurisdiction.

The terrorists carried out the death sentence with utter success on Monday, April 3, at 7 PM, in a street in Galata [modern Karaköy, in Beyoğlu (Pera) Istanbul]. As the spy Ardashes, mortally wounded, rolled around on the ground in the throes of death, the police ran to his aid and transported him to a hospital, where a few hours later he gave up his black spirit to Sultan Hamid.... Despite many arrests, not one bit of evidence was found. The terrorists who carried out the death sentence freely move about the city, thanks to the munificence of His Highness the Sultan.

From Droshak, *July 1895*

HAROUTIUN SHAHRIGIAN (NITRA, ADOM)
1860–1915

BORN IN SHABIN-KARAHISAR, Shahrigian graduated from Galatasaray College (high school) in Constantinople and then from the Faculty of Law of the University of Constantinople. He joined the Dashnaktsoutiun, eventually becoming a member of the ARF Bureau.

Shahrigian served as a lawyer in Trebizond from 1889 to 1895 and was often called upon to defend Armenian political prisoners.

At the same time, Shahrigian engaged in various ARF and civic activities.

Himself arrested by Ottoman authorities during the 1895–96 massacres, Shahrigian managed to escape and crossed over into Transcaucasia. In 1897, on behalf of the ARF Bureau, he settled the internal squabbles in the Dashnaktsakan organization of Iran, in Salmast, and gave approval for launching the Khanasor Expedition.

The Second World Congress elected him to the Eastern Bureau (1898), which he represented in the Potorik Committee (which raised funds from wealthy Armenians for the ARF's militant activities from 1901 to 1903). During the Armeno-Tatar conflict, from 1905 to 1906, the Bureau dispatched Shahrigian to the northern Caucasus to secure funds for the purchase of ammunition.

In 1908, Shahrigian settled in Constantinople after the proclamation of the Ottoman Constitution. He attempted to convince the government to build railways in the eastern provinces of Turkey (Western Armenia), to no avail. He served as a member of the Armenian National Assembly and wrote articles for *Azatamart* and other Dashnak publications. He also authored separate works on the Ottoman Empire and Ottoman reforms.

Endowed with a strong, original personality, Shahrigian was a prominent figure in national affairs and in the ARF. He fell victim to the 1915 Genocide. He was 55 years old.

*

The future, then, lies not in fusion—assimilation—but in a policy of unity, or more correctly, in a policy of pluralistic unity. Erase variety in nature, in the universe, make the universe uniform, and you will have erased the beauty of nature, its harmony, its life. Variety in nature, which seems to put every element at odds with another, actually, through harmony, forms the greatness of the perpetual motion of the universe.

From Mer Havadamke *(Our Credo), 1908, republished in 1981, Beirut*

HOVNAN DAVTIAN (HONAN NANOYIAN)
1865–1918

BORN IN SHOUSHI, Karabagh, Davtian was one of the most outstanding and idealistic figures of the ARF's first generation.

He completed his secondary education at the Tiflis Nersisian College and studied political and social sciences at the University of Geneva.

In 1891, invited to Tabriz, Persia, to teach, he joined the group led by Hovsep "Ishkhan" Arghoutian and Nikol Douman. In 1892, he attended the First World Congress of the ARF, where, with Zavarian, he hotly defended organizational decentralization.

After a few years of teaching in Tabriz, he returned to Geneva to continue his studies. He worked on *Droshak* with Rostom and also during Rostom's absence (1895–1896). In the summer of 1896, when the assassination of the Sultan was being planned, he went to Constantinople; he returned to Geneva after the failed attempt. He was back in Tabriz in 1898 and in Switzerland once more in 1900. The following year he returned to Tiflis and remained for a fairly long period. He was the editor of *Harach* (Forward) from 1905 to 1906.

He was back in Tabriz form 1908 to 1913 as director of the Central School. Subsequently, he returned to Geneva, where he remained. He died there of tuberculosis in August of 1918, at the age of 53.

Honan's wife, Hortense Berchier, a Swiss citizen, spoke and wrote Armenian fluently. She was Honan's life companion, sharing his concerns, sentiments, and commitment toward the Armenian people. She also died of tuberculosis, in 1917, in Geneva.

The following remarks by Honan were made during the height of the Armenian revolutionary movement, in the mid-1890s.

*

Although we consider the Eastern Question a powerful weapon, we do not think that we can, with this single weapon, achieve our aspirations. We have always said that no hope should be placed on diplomacy; it is not a friend of the freedom of peoples. But powerful revolutionary movements force it to make concessions; and if it does make a concession, that, for us, is a step forward—nothing more.

Diplomacy never makes a concession easily, as the evidence of the most recent events attests; through cunning games and maneuvers it attempts to throw dust into the eyes of the people, as it has done up to this day.... We must learn from the past, and we must be very careful regarding the most recent games, the objective of which may simply be to calm the disquiet being felt....

So that, this time around, all the work and sacrifices do not go to waste, we must continue the fight—the only means of forcing diplomacy to take into consideration the demands of the discontented people. And when the demands of the Armenian people are taken into consideration, when it takes a forward step, an ample and favorable arena will be created for revolutionary activity; by gathering greater strength and having a broader realm for activity, it will become possible to succeed in our sacred goal the liberation of Turkish Armenia… for which the Armenian Revolutionary Federation struggles today.

Once more we appeal to the Armenian people. The present moment is advantageous for our cause. To become careless now is to make the greatest of historical mistakes, to betray the cause of the people of Turkish Armenia, and to insult the memory of thousands of martyrs.

From "Nerka Ropen," (The Present Moment) Droshak, *No. 19, 1895*

AVETIS AHARONIAN
1866–1948

A HARONIAN WAS BORN in Igdirmava, a village of Igdir, in the Surmalu region, at the foot of Mount Ararat. He received his secondary education at the Gevorgian College (Seminary) of Ejmiatzin. He later attended the Sorbonne, in Paris, and the University of Lausanne, in Switzerland. He was a prolific writer and activist, and a member of the ARF Bureau.

Aharonian worked for *Droshak* and headed the editorial staff of the *Mourch* (Hammer) and *Harach* newspapers in Transcaucasia. He was also the principal of the Nersisian School in Tiflis, Georgia.

In 1909, toward the end of the Tsarist persecution of revolutionaries, he was imprisoned for two years by Russian authorities for being an ARF leader. He returned to Switzerland after his release from prison.

During the years of Armenian independence, Aharonian headed the delegation of the Armenian Republic to Constantinople, and also at the Peace Conference in Paris, where he signed the Treaty of Sevres on behalf of the Republic of Armenia.

His last words, translated below, were spoken in February 1948, in Marseille, France, at a Hamazkayin Cultural Association gathering of some two thousand people, at which he was the main speaker. He suffered a stroke on stage and died two months later, in Paris, at the age of 82.

*

Armenian people, understand that this a waystation. Believe that you will return to the land of your forefathers, to the land of brave men. We have come here in order to not stay, we have come in order to return...

Know, Armenian people, that... you have something to say to this ignoble world. I do not compare my lofty and wise nation to any other. Armenian people and youth, be well convinced that you have no need to bow before any other nation.

For us to know who we were and who we are, it is enough to see the ruins of Ani.... Such glory and honor, what a magnificent demonstration of the culture and civilization of the Bagratouni dynasty... What arches, what churches. After seeing Ani, when under a picture I read the line "Past and present Armenia," my spirit soars for a moment, knowing that all those temples were built under the bellows of wars... Oh, that's when we understand the worth of our forefathers, of their creations, of their armies of brave men.

Excerpt from speech, Marseille, France. February 11, 1948

GENERAL ANTRANIG (ANTRANIG OZANIAN)
1866–1927

ANTRANIG WAS BORN in Shabin-Karahisar, Western Armenia, where he attended the Mousheghian School and received early training in carpentry, his father's trade. He began his revolutionary activity in Sepasdia province in 1888, and joined the Dashnaktsoutiun in 1892, in Constantinople.

Soon after joining the ARF, Antranig returned to the interior provinces, where he defended Armenian villages in the Moush-Sasoun district in 1895–96. He crossed over to Van with group leader Vazgen in July 1897 and then moved on to Akhlat and Sasoun, where he stayed until 1904 as a rank-and-file fighter. He took on a greater role there after the assassination of fedayi leader Aghbiur Serop in 1900.

With Kevork Chavoush and Magar, he avenged Serop by killing the Kurdish executioner, Bshareh Khalil. With the blessing of the Central Committee of Moush, he and Kevork Chavoush organized and led the fighting at the besieged Arakelots monastery (near Moush) in 1901, donning the uniforms of Turkish officers in order to escape.

In 1903, he was appointed commander of the Dashnaktsakan forces in Sasoun and led the 1904 uprising. Immediately thereafter, he withdrew to Vaspourakan with his fedayis and eventually reached Iran.

A participant in many high-level ARF assemblies, Antranig attended the Council of ARF Representatives at Geneva in 1905. He then settled in Bulgaria, where he played an active role in establishing the ARF military academy.

He took part in the Fourth ARF World Congress in Vienna in 1907 and was elected a member of the ARF's Demonstrative Body, which was in charge of demonstrative actions (propaganda by deed). An audacious, enterprising military leader, Antranig was also intractable by nature and began having difficulties with the party soon after, citing philosophical differences. He nevertheless continued to work within the ARF until the days of the Independent Republic, but made a final break from the party thereafter.

Antranig fought alongside the Bulgarians in the Balkan War of 1912, also identifying himself with Macedonian liberation movement. He went to the Caucasus in 1914 and was given command of the First Armenian Volunteer Regiment on the Caucasian front. Under the supreme command of General Nazarbegian (Nazarbegov), Antranig won the battle of Dilman. His forces joined with the Armenian legion in expelling the Turks from south of Lake Van but were forced to retreat by a Turkish counteroffensive in July, 1915. His unit was dissolved by the authorities in 1916.

Promoted to the rank of division general in 1917, Antranig led a Western Armenian division which attempted to hold off the eastward advance of Turkish forces. Forced to evacuate Erzurum in March 1918, he resigned his command and left for Tiflis the same month. He then formed a new Western Armenian unit but did not participate in the decisive battles around Sardarabad in May 1918.

After independence, Antranig had misunderstandings with the Republic's government, partly over the decision to sign the Treaty of Batum in June 1918. He remained in the Transcaucasus for the next few years, leading Armenian military resistance to Tatar incursions in Zangezour, Nakhijevan, and Karabagh. About to retake Karabagh in December 1918, Antranig was halted by a message from the British regional commander, who guaranteed a peaceful solution to the question. The situation was subsequently left unresolved, resulting in Karabagh's exclusion from Armenia's borders.

Forced by British pressure to disband his forces, Antranig left the Caucasus in 1919. He first went to Paris and London, trying to persuade the Allies to occupy Turkish Armenia. He went on to the US, where he raised funds for the Armenian army. He died in 1927, in Fresno, California.

His remains were buried in the Père Lachaise cemetery in Paris, after Soviet authorities refused to allow his interment in Soviet

Armenia. His remains were eventually transferred to Armenia, in 1990.

*

Not the Turkish rifles, not the cold nor the wind could frighten or dim the flame that resided in our hearts, when only yesterday we had buried our dear Ghazar amid tears and revenge. It would have been necessary to kill, to kill repeatedly, to dissolve the vengeance for all those who had fallen. Like a storm, thousands of bullets were whistling by our heads, in front of our feet, but the monastery stood there, majestic and strong. We never weakened, never succumbed, and with our courageous stand were able to demoralize the already weakened and discouraged arms of our enemy, inflicting many casualties.

Excerpt from an interview with Gen. Antranig regarding the defense of the Arakelots monastery. Printed in L. Liuledjian, Antranigi Pernov Arakelots Vanki Grive yev Khalil Begi Sbannoutiune, *Beirut, 1966*

GAREGIN KHAZHAK (CHAKALIAN)
1867–1915

BORN GAREGIN CHAKALIAN in Alexandropol (Giumri, later Leninakan), Khazhak graduated from the Faculty of Social Sciences at the University of Geneva with a degree in sociology.

In 1894, he returned to Geneva from Baku, where he had joined the ranks of the ARF, and began to work for *Droshak,* the central party organ.

In 1895 he was sent on an organizing mission to the Balkans, where he soon became one of the leading pioneers of the ARF.

Later (1897–98) he was sent on a similar mission to Smyrna, then Egypt.

From 1898 to 1903 he was a member of the ARF's Responsible Body for Constantinople.

Returning to the Transcaucasus in 1903, he taught at the Nersisian College in Ejmiatzin and contributed to *Mshak* in Tiflis. From 1906 to 1911, in Tiflis, he was a member of the editorial team of *Harach* and *Alik* with Avetis Aharonian and Yeghishe Topjian.

He settled in Constantinople in 1911–1912 and became the director of the national school in the Samatia district, working for the newspaper *Azatamart* at the same time.

One of the most brilliant representatives of the Dashnaktsakan intelligentsia, Khazhak was also among the first victims of the Armenian Genocide, in 1915. He was 48 years old.

*

My dear Shoushanik, sweet companion of my life:

Today I can write with assurance that they are taking us to Tigranakert [Diyarbekir] to hand us over to the military court, under the suspicion that we want to start an insurrection in the land. And that means they are taking us there to hang.

Therefore, my beautiful companion, when by some miracle this letter reaches you, I will have ceased to exist. My dearest, carry out my last request:

1. Take the children and leave this accursed and immoral country; settle in our old home and dedicate yourself to the education of our children.

2. Keep this piece of paper, and when the children become of age give it to them; let them read it and follow their father's footsteps.

I will soon have lived 48 years, but I have not yet lived 48 days with moments of rest; the damned fate of the Armenian people has pursued me, and it seems it has focused on my comrades and me. To live like this is bitter, very bitter, and to die like this is especially bitter. I am angry but not despondent. Be certain that when facing the gallows, I will have two pictures before my eyes: first, the suffering of my people; second, yours, my Nunu's, my Alo's and, alas my third child's. Will I cry or smile, I don't know… If only, before I hang, my heart, which has begun to throb so loudly, would burst… How terrifying it is not to see the birth of one's child and to be hanged… and to be hanged so treacherously like this, without any just cause, merely by suspicion. My beautiful Shoushanik, when my children are grown, give them these few lines… let them dedicate themselves to [assuaging] the pain of their people and nation.

There is no tear in my eyes, perhaps because, as a human being, I still harbor hopes that I will live…. Although I have not participated in any practical work in Turkey, I will nevertheless hang, because I am a known Dashnaktsakan….

Goodbye by beautiful companion, goodbye by angels Nunush and Alo, and goodbye my third and unknown child, whose birth into the world I will not see. If only we would be the last victims sacrificed on the altar of the Armenian people; if only with our blood this wretched nation would finally find its rest. Goodbye. I pour all my soul in my kiss that I place on this piece of paper…. It is as if the prophecy my mother made in 1892, "You will die in a dark jail," is coming true. God, how bitter the thought of dying far away from loved ones. My kisses, again and again, to all of you. Let our children walk the path I traveled, a bitter but noble path.

Your Khazhak

July 4, 1915

NIKOL DOUMAN
(NIKOGHAYOS TER HOVHANNISIAN)
1867–1914

BORN IN GHSHLAGH, in Karabagh, Douman received his education at the diocesan school of Shoushi.

From 1891 to 1894, he pursued organizational activities and taught in the Armenian schools of Tabriz and Salmast.

From 1894 onward, he moved between Salmast and Vaspourakan, engaging Turkish troops and Kurdish armed bands in battles that have remained famous, including those of Derik, Sara, and Boghaz-Kyasan, after which the Kurds conferred upon him the nickname "Douman" (storm).

Both a fighter and a strategist, Nikol Douman was one of the principal organizers of the Expedition of Khanasor in 1897.

He then settled in Baku, where he was mainly involved in training young Dashnaktsakans in underground and military activities.

In 1904 he tried in vain to reach the insurgents of Sasoun to reinforce their ranks, but his armed band was dispersed after violent border clashes.

During the fighting between Armenians and Tatars (Azeris) in 1905, Nikol Douman was appointed commander-in-chief of operations in Yerevan province and the Ararat Plain.

In 1907, he wrote the manual *Nakhagitz Zhoghovrdakan Inknapashtpanoutian* (Outline for Popular Self-Defense).

Then, as the commanding officer of a group of 100 men, he successfully secured the defense of Tabriz during the Persian Constitutional Revolution. In 1910, he took part in the International Socialist Congress held in Copenhagen.

In September 1914, his health hopelessly deteriorating, and unable to join his comrades in battle, Nikol Douman took his own life. He was 47 years old.

*

Life plays strange games. One of those games is the reason for the necessity of this "manual" [the Outline for Popular Self-Defense].

Immediately after the Armenian-Turkish [Azeri] clashes in the Caucasus, my comrades proposed that I prepare this self-defense manual.

I was uncertain...

I was uncertain because I knew that this booklet would contain bloody lessons.

Blood is not odd for me, nor is it alien.

But I perfectly understand and completely sympathize only when that blood flows from the veins of governments that torment the people.

But here, in this manual?

A brother is taught to dip his hands into the blood of his brother, neighbor to stand against neighbor, one nation to clash with another...

That is why I was uncertain. But, in the end, implacable reality won.

In Turkey, there are muted whispers that forebode terrifying reactionary developments. In Persia, there are frequent clashes between the opposing currents of autocracy and constitutionalisrn. And in Russia, who knows what surprises are being prepared?

Uncertainty is now a crime. Every person who perceives the seriousness of the situation must speak, must encourage the [abovementioned] three segments of the Armenian people to prepare for self-defense.

And, fatefully, they must prepare.

But...

But I would feel spiritually consoled and morally rewarded if one yearned-for day... all those military preparations were aimed at the monstrous foreheads of those treacherous governments and sanctioned parasites that, by poisoning nations, have placed us before the dark necessity of composing fratricidal lessons.

From the Epilogue of Outline for Popular Self-Defense, *1907*

LEVON SHANT (LEVON SEGHPOSIAN)
1869–1951

BORN IN SCUTARI (Üsküdar), in Constantinople, Levon Shant attended the Üsküdar Armenian school until age 14. He then attended the Gevorgian College of Ejmiatzin, from which he graduated in 1891. He returned that year as a teacher to Constantinople, where his first literary work was published by the local *Hayrenik* daily.

He furthered his studies in Germany and Switzerland (1892–1899), where he studied science, child psychology, education, literature, and history. He joined the ARF in its early days and did much work in the fields of culture, society, and politics.

Upon returning to Constantinople, Shant became a leading figure in Armenian theater. In addition to his work as a playwright, he was a poet and teacher.

He was vice-president of parliament in the Armenian Republic, and in April 1920 he led the Armenian delegation to Moscow, seeking entente with the Soviet regime.

After the Soviet takeover of Armenia, He settled in Cairo, Egypt, and in 1928 co-founded the Hamazkayin Cultural Association. Together with Nikol Aghbalian, in 1930 he founded the Hamazkayin Jemaran (College) in Beirut, serving as its principal. Despite his advanced age, he ran the school expertly until his death in 1951, ever active in intellectual and literary matters.

Among his best-known works are his plays, most of which had historical or philosophical themes: *Hin Asdvadzner* (Ancient Gods, 1909), *Gaysre* (The Emperor, 1914), *Ingadz Perti Ishkhanouhin* (The Princess of the Fallen Castle, 1921), and *Oshin Bayl* (1929). He also penned essays and booklets, including *Azkoutiune Himk Martgayin Ungeroutian* (Nationhood as the Basis of Human Society, 1922) and *Mer Angakhoutiune* (Our Independence, 1925).

Hin Asdvadzner premiered in Tiflis in 1913 and shook up the Armenian literary world. It was translated into English, German, Italian, French, and Russian. Konstantin Stanislavski directed a Russian production of it in 1917. *Gaysre* and *Hin Asdvadzner* are among the most frequently staged Armenian dramas.

*

As we have seen, our neighboring peoples in the Caucasus also tend inexorably toward independence, and with more emphasis and urgency than we, because they are more concentrated and dense in population and because they can rely on Turkey. But, for them, a major prerequisite for reaching their aim is the position that we adopt: If we do not move as they do and walk in stride with them, we become an extremely large obstacle.

With our indecision—rather, more correctly, our opposition—we deal a blow not only to our own vital interests but also to theirs, because in such an environment of resolve and passion it is impossible to remain immobile and "prudent"—a non-participant.

And very rightly, very naturally, we will be considered by our neighbors as Russia's ally and the enemy of their own existence and aspirations. And so that they may reach their aim, first they will attempt to diminish and render useless the enemy that is within them, beside them, and at their rear. They will also consider us the cause of their every defeat and failure, and will therefore wreak their revenge and hatred upon us: Resentment and hatred against the strong is always taken out on the week and the defenseless—that is an ancient principle. They will do whatever they can to strangle us morally, economically, and physically....

Nor can we expect respect and friendship from the Russians in return for our having been laid low and persecuted—for the services we have provided. In political life, as in our individual lives, respect and friendship are attained only if we have value and self-respect. Russia, after having turned us into an obedient tool and pitted us against our neighbors, will, during moments of reckoning, always take the side of the Tatars and the Georgians; because the Georgian and the Tatar, as a result of their very resistance and demands, will represent a force that Russia has to take into account when making its decisions. And what need for Russia to worry too much about their "friend," the pitiable Armenians, who have resigned from exercising their own willpower and who rely entirely on Russia's arms and fortunes for their own defense....

Whoever, deep in his heart, has not irrevocably resigned from his homeland, from his national existence and identity, from the Armenian nation, must simply and clearly grasp that there is no benefit to be had from others, nor is there respite to be had from others. If we want to live as a nation, to endure and to develop, our only outlet is independence. There is no other way.

From Mer Angakhoutiune *(Our Independence),*
Hairenik Press, 1925

YEPREM KHAN (DAVTIAN)
1871–1912

BORN IN THE village of Barsoum, in Gandzak (present-day Gyanje, in Azerbaijan), Karabagh, Yeprem took part in the Koukounian (Gougounian) Expedition in 1890 and was subsequently exiled by Russian authorities to Sakhalin Island. He eventually escaped, reaching Atrpatakan (Iranian Azerbaijan). There, he joined the ARF and became an active fieldworker. He also took part in the Khanasor Expedition of 1897.

In 1899 he assassinated the informer Zakeh, who had been

responsible for the massacre of nine ARF fedayis in the village of Mahlam. He was a member of the ARF Central Committee of Atrpatakan for several terms of office.

Yeprem earned fame especially in the days of the Iranian Constitutional Revolution, when with a small band of men he took the northern Iranian towns of Rasht, Enzeli, Kharzan, and Ghazvin.

Later, at the head of an ever-growing number of Armenian and Iranian revolutionaries, he entered Tehran in triumph against the anti-constitutional Iranian forces and was appointed chief of police there.

With a group of ARF fedayis under the command of Keri and Dashnaktsakan Khecho, Yeprem continued fighting against the anti-constitutional forces of Iran. He was later granted the rank of "Sardar" (military commander) and awarded a gem-studded sword and a pension.

He was killed on April 25, 1912, along with Nikol of Karabagh, during the battle of Sourjieh, near Hamadan (ancient Ecbatana), while attempting to recover the body of a fallen comrade during fighting against counter-revolutionary forces. He was buried in the yard of Tehran's Haykazian School (at present, Davtian School). He was 44 years old.

Yeprem is considered a national hero of the Iranian liberation movement.

*

A Decision of the Fourth World Congress of the ARF

Noting that the present Persian movement may become a great social phenomenon of popular awakening both for Persia and the East, and finding it desirable, from the viewpoint of both Armenians and all mankind, that the movement spread and expand…

The World Congress prescribes that the Dashnaktsakan organizational bodies and individuals in Persia aid, through all means, the development of that movement, inserting in the Persian awakening the liberal, democratic, and working class spirit reflected in the Constitution of the ARF.

1907, Vienna

ARMEN GARO (GAREGIN PASTERMAJIAN)
1872–1923

BORN IN GARIN (Erzurum), Armen Garo graduated from the Sanasarian School there and attended the School of Agronomy in Nancy, France, in 1894.

Strongly attracted to the Armenian revolutionary movement, with a few friends he went to Geneva (*Droshak*) in 1895 to join the ARF. Soon thereafter he was sent to Egypt, Cyprus, then Constantinople, where he played a leading role in the seizure of the Ottoman Bank on August 14, 1896.

He and Hrach Tiryakian led negotiations with European ambassadors to end the Armenian massacres unleashed by the Sultan and to ensure the safe passage of the Armenian revolutionaries who had captured the Ottoman Bank.

He returned to Switzerland and resumed his studies, graduating in 1900 with a PhD in chemistry. In 1898, the Second World Congress of the ARF elected him a member of its Western Bureau.

In 1901 he settled in Tiflis. There, he led the defense of the mostly Armenian-populated city during the Armeno-Tatar (Azeri) confrontations of 1905–1906.

After the proclamation of the Ottoman Constitution in 1908, Armen Garo was elected a member of the Ottoman Parliament in 1909. He settled in Constantinople, then Garin.

In the autumn of 1914, he returned to the Caucasus. There, he played an important role in organizing the Armenian Volunteer Movement as General Dro's associate and was appointed deputy commander of the Second Regiment.

After the independence of Armenia in 1918, he was appointed a member of the Armenian National Delegation at the Paris peace talks, and then ambassador of the Armenian Republic in Washington, DC, from 1919 to 1921.

He played a leading role in the planning and implementation of the ARF's Operation Nemesis, the plan to assassinate Turkish leaders responsible for the Armenian Genocide. He died in Geneva in March, 1923. He was 51 years old.

*

We are in the bank. The time is approximately 1:30. The door is half-open. Standing directly across from the door, we are firing—Misak of Moush, Rouben, Mkhitar, and I on one side, and three comrades on the other. The smoke from the handguns has already filled the lobby; we can see nothing through the door; only the constant roar of rifles lets us know that there are large numbers of troops outside....

As soon as we turned again toward the door... a terrible explosion. It was Misak of Moush. While taking the bombs from his belt, he was shot and wounded in the leg and released a bomb. The scene was terrifying; he was lying on the stone floor, his left forearm shattered, his right arm torn to bits, hanging from his shoulder by a few strands of muscle, his face bloody, his clothes ripped apart....

We heard from outside: "Men, go in, go in," and saw the tips of bayonets shining through the smoke.... The rounds fired from six or seven handguns drove back the bayonets... [and] the explosion of five bombs cleared the street for a while.

As Mkhitar and I, carrying more bombs, turned toward the window, Misak, with his frightful appearance, on his knees, neck bent, popped up in front of us: "*Baron jan, kiz ghurban, meg ghurshun esdeghits*" (Sir, please, one bullet, aimed here) he said, pointing toward his breast with the remainder of his right arm. I began to shake with my whole being. I can't say for certain what I felt at that moment. I remember only that I put the wooden part of my handgun in my mouth, bit on it with all my strength, and looked away. Again he came in front of me, dragging his bloody leg on the floor. He repeated his request... his voice, his appearance demoralized me completely. To reject him was unmerciful; each second brought terrible torture for him.... I don't know why I didn't empty my gun into his tortured chest, and I turned to Mkhitar: "Mkhitar *jan*, free the poor boy." Misak immediately turned his bloodied face toward him and said, "*Mkhitar jan, kiz madagh, meg ghurshun.*" Mkhitar, completely pale, with shaking hand pointed the handgun toward his chest…. Misak, a trace of satisfaction on his face, pulled back his dismembered arms as if to make his comrade's task easier. Eyes filled with tears, Mkhitar looked at me, "No, I can't," and turning to Misak, weeping, said, "Misak *jan,* go stand in front of that second window, and one of the bullets from the soldiers will take you."…A few seconds later Misak was kneeling in front of the window, his head and a part of his chest sticking out the window…. He yelled in a loud voice and poured out a string of curses at the soldiers. Fifteen minutes passed, and despite… the hundreds of bullets flying by him, none killed him.

Suddenly he stopped his shouting and turned toward us, "Boys, get ready, *bashibozuk* [irregulars] are coming."… When the mob attacked the door, six of us on the first floor… and [five] comrades from the roof sent a downpour of bombs…. The heart-wrenching screams of the wounded, the crash of window glass from the building across the street, and the dynamite's blue smoke rising toward the sky shook me for a moment: We were dealing with human lives… Who gave us this right… But why did they start it… Who were the ones, months before, who caused rivers of blood to flow…. I looked out the window… bodies… the remainder of the mob fleeing in terror….

In a moment of terrible silence, I hear Misak. I turn to my right. His bloodied arms hanging like rags out the window, waving them at the fleeing mob, a horrifying smile on his face, he cursed with his already hoarse, half-dead voice.

Oh, that smile of his…

If one day in this struggle for survival the time comes for our afflicted Armenian nation to die, to disappear from the face of the earth, if it does so without that last smile of Misak of Moush... a thousand pities for the blood it has shed.

From Droshak, *1900*

LIPARIT NAZARIANTS
1872–1947

BORN IN THE Chatal Oghli village of Lori, Nazariants moved at an early age to Yerevan, where he attended Yerevan's Russian School (Gymnasium). He received his higher education first at Moscow University, where he specialized in law, and later at Berlin University, where he specialized in philosophy, graduating in 1901.

Joining the ARF during his years in Europe. Nazariants became particularly active in galvanizing the Armenian student movement in Europe at the turn of the century.

In 1905, he returned to the Caucasus, spending some time in Baku, then Tiflis, where he became part of the editorial staff of the ARE publication *Harach*. Journalism was to remain an integral part of his activities for the rest of his life.

Following the establishment of the constitutional order in the Ottoman Empire, Nazariants moved to Constantinople, where he became part of the editorial staff of *Azatamart*. Before the outbreak of World War I, he moved to Germany to serve as a correspondent for several European newspapers. During the war, he was sent back to Constantinople on behalf of an Armeno-German association. Soon after, he left Turkey to become editor of *Hayastan* in Sofia, Bulgaria.

Nazariants was a prominent diplomatic figure during Armenia's years of independence, serving for a time as a consular official in Berlin.

He, along with Dr. Hagop Zavrian (Zavriev) and Artashes Chilingirian (Rouben Darbinian), formed the official delegation that traveled to Moscow in 1920, seeking the diplomatic recognition of the Republic of Armenia from the Soviets. Upon arrival in Moscow, Zavrian and Nazariants were imprisoned, whereas Darbinian escaped. Nazariants and Zavrian were both released months later, with Zavrian dying shortly thereafter from the ill treatment he had received in prison.

Upon the fall of the Armenian Republic, Nazariants moved again to Europe. An active participant in Operation Nemesis (the movement to punish those responsible for the Armenian Genocide), he also served as one of the defense lawyers during the 1921 Berlin trial of Soghomon Tehlirian, who had assassinated Talaat Pasha. Tehlirian was eventually acquitted.

In 1928, Nazariants moved to Egypt. There, he would spend the rest of his days working primarily as an editorial associate for the ARF newspaper *Houssaper* (Bringer of Hope). He also had a substantial literary output that included plays and translations.

*

Beginning in the morning of April 24, the entire police force of Constantinople was put into motion. They began making arrests, one by one, from pre-arranged lists. That night the main act of treachery took place, continuing until morning. It is true that for days prior to the event ominous whispers had made the rounds, hut it was hard to envision such mass arrests that took no account of citizenship, class, or political allegiances…. [Y]et there is one thing you [Turks] should know. The Armenians are accustomed to prisons and exile, and they are accustomed to going to the gallows with smiling faces. In this lies their strength, and it is because of this strength that they will one day reach their goals, namely to be able—in unfettered fashion—in harmony with other peoples, to live and prosper in a truly free homeland, where now only sad memories of you [Turks] will have remained.

From Droshak, *May 11, 1988 (likely republished from* Houssaper*)*

MARIAM MAKARIAN (MARO)
1872–1896

BORN IN DERBENT, in Daghestan, Russia (northwest of Baku), and orphaned at an early age, Maro was raised by her brothers and educated at the local secondary school. While a student, she actively participated in gatherings organized by activist-patriotic groups. She joined the Dashnaktsoutiun at its inception.

In 1894 she moved to Tabriz as a teacher and revolutionary fieldworker and was elected to the local ARF body.

She taught needle-lace to young Armenian women, also forming reading and discussion groups in which she read the *Droshak* and discussed social and national issues of the day.

She participated in the work of transporting arms and ammunition to Turkish Armenia, and her home became a veritable arms depot, as well as a hideout for revolutionaries on the run. When working in the effort to transport arms, she met and became engaged to Aristakes (Karo) Zorian, Rostom's younger brother and a founder of the ARF's weapons foundry in Tabriz.

In 1896, Maro went to Salmast (Iran) to help in the preparations for the Khanasor expedition against the Mazrik tribe of Kurds. In Salmast, she saw that Karo was hesitant to participate in the expedition. Ascribing that hesitation to his love for her, Maro found herself in emotional turmoil and steadily fell into deep depression.

On December 2, 1896, Maro committed suicide. She left behind a letter (excerpt below), not addressed to anyone but certainly meant for Karo.

Karo took part in the Khanasor expedition on July 25, 1897. He was killed in the fighting, one of only a few Armenian casualties that day.

*

You who cast the work of Armenia's liberation above my and your personal happiness, you who sacrificed your love to a higher idealistic love, now carry out your word—place your life as sacrifice on the sacred altar of the homeland. Like Papken Siuni [of Bank Ottoman], fill yourself with lethal vengeance. Carry out my last bequest, only thus can my bones find rest in my grave. I had enough courage to be able to burn all the ships behind you; henceforth, you are completely free. Go to your work. Forgive me. A thousand kisses. My last greetings to all our comrades.

From Maro's last letter

*

It is a regular day. The sun is hot enough to burn, although a white sheet of snow still covers everything in a thick layer. The bells toll sadly. The men and women of the village have surrounded a red coffin that the fedayis are carrying toward the hilltop, to the cemetery. There were among them representatives from as far away as Ardos and the Caucasus.... They were burying their dear "Tato," who had sacrificed so much for the homeland's freedom-fighters and soldiers. They sense that no one will take the place of their sister. Tears are falling in streams on creased faces, coarsened fists unable to wipe them.

From Droshak, 22 February 1897

MIKAYEL VARANDIAN (HOVHANNISIAN)
1872–1934

VARANDIAN WAS BORN in Karabagh, in Varanda, from which his pseudonym is derived. He attended the diocesan school of Shoushi and thereafter studied social sciences and philosophy at several German universities, then graduated from the University of Geneva.

Varandian lived mainly in Geneva and Paris and was a member of the *Droshak* editorial team and a party administrator and archivist.

At the ARF's Fourth World Congress (1904) he was elected a member of the party's Western Bureau.

As the main theoretician/ideologist of the ARF, Varandian represented Dashnaktsoutiun at the Second (Socialist) International, attending its Copenhagen conference in 1910. He also cultivated links with European socialist leaders of the day.

During independence, he was elected to the Parliament of the Armenian Republic. He served as Armenia's ambassador to Italy from 1918 to 1920.

Varandian was a prolific writer. Among his books are *The Prehistory of the Armenian Movement, Currents, Protest in Recent History, The Reawakening Homeland and Our Role, Dashnaktsoutiun and its Adversaries, Simon Zavarian, Mourad*, and other works, in particular his two-volume *History of the Armenian Revolutionary Federation*.

Varandian died in France of a heart attack. He was 60 years old.

*

Protest in the name of political-constitutional liberty, protest in the name of social equality, these are the two great axes around which human history revolves, especially most recent history.

Within the political movements are the national-liberation movements, the heroic revolts of enslaved and subject peoples against foreign and tyrannical domination. There is no other subject as moving, as engaging. Unfortunately, our calamitous reality does not allow one to ponder such subjects at length. Today there is still apparent interest in them, but tomorrow, who knows; the ill-fated wave of our national welfare may once again go crashing down into the mysterious unknown, may once again divert our attention from such exercises...

Nevertheless, it is necessary to present, albeit briefly, the history of at least the last century to the Armenian reader. For even in moments of crisis, knowledge of history is perhaps the supreme remedy for our grief and our wounds; perhaps the study of exhilarating and inspiring pan-human protest can dissipate the fog of hopelessness, dangerous hesitation, and fatalistic abandonment that periodically gathers on the Armenian horizon...

From the "Foreword" to Protest in Recent History,
Geneva, 1911

SEBOUH (ARSHAG NERSESIAN)
1872–1940

BORN IN THE village of Varzahan, in Papert (Bayburt), Western Armenia, Sebouh showed early aptitude as a craftsman. He received his secondary education in Trebizond.

He joined the Hnchak party in Constantinople in 1889 and participated in the 1892 demonstration at Kum-Kapu, protesting Ottoman oppression. Afterward, he left for the Crimea, then the Caucasus, where he joined the ARF in 1894. He became a party organizer in his hometown and took part in groups that transported arms to Western Armenia.

In 1903, Sebouh went to Sasoun and joined Torkom's "Mrrik" group. He later became one of the leaders of the 1904 Sasoun rebellion. Seriously wounded in Sasoun, he remained in Akhlat for a time, then Vaspourakan (Van).

During the Armeno-Tatar conflict of 1905–1906, Sebouh fought in Nakhijevan. He also took part in the Iranian Constitutional Revolution (1905–1907). He attended the ARF's Fourth World Congress in Vienna, in 1907.

After the proclamation of the Ottoman Constitution in 1908, the Ottoman authorities ceased to persecute former revolutionaries, and Sebouh returned to his birthplace, where he lived for a time.

In 1914–1915, Sebouh fought in the battles of Khoy and Dilman at the side of Antranig. Later, he was part of the Armeno-Russian forces that liberated Garin (Erzurum) in 1918. At the head of an ARF formation, he took part in the decisive battle of Sardarabad in 1918. He then went on to Baku to protect the Armenians under siege there and to defend the city against Ottoman forces.

After the independence of Armenia, Sebouh bore the rank of brigadier general in the Armenian Army. At the head of a special unit, in May 1920, he suppressed the Bolshevik insurrection in Shirak. He also fought in the Armeno-Turkish War of 1920.

After the Sovietization of Armenia, he left for the United States, where he died at the age of 68.

*

[In 1917–1918] the situation was sad and grim.... Where was that great military leader who enjoyed the sympathy of the people and could lead it?

There was no one. We had no one. If there was a military man whom we could call "great," he was General Nazarbegov, who was sitting in Tiflis and did not want to come to this side [Western Armenia]. What is he thinking and why does he not come? No one knows. Perhaps he, with his authority and impartiality, could put an end to the Russian-Armenian vs. Turkish-Armenian problem. And if there was to be an improvement in our military situation, only Gen. Nazarbegov could accomplish it.

The greatest source of adversity and misfortune for us is this sectarian passion. The day that it ends, so will our misery; the Armenian people will be freed from the oppression of their own passions, as well as external enemies.

From Pages From My Memoirs, *Hairenik Press, Boston, 1925*

HAMO OHANJANIAN (MHERIAN)
1873–1947

B ORN IN AKHALKALAK, present-day Georgia, Ohanjanian received his elementary education locally, and his secondary schooling at Tiflis High School. He went on to Moscow as a medical student, and later to Switzerland to further his medical studies. He joined the Dashnaktsoutiun while a student in Moscow.

In 1898, he established a branch of the ARF Red Cross. In 1902, he settled in Tiflis and soon became a leading figure there, enjoying unanimous esteem. While in Tiflis, he established the ARF newspaper *Harach*.

A member of the Eastern Bureau of the ARF from 1905 onward, he took part in that capacity in the ARF's Geneva Council, where he ardently defended the "Plan of Action for Transcaucasia." During that time, he also coordinated relations with Russian and Georgian revolutionaries throughout the duration of the Armeno-Tatar conflict.

Enjoying the esteem of Dashnaktsakan combatants as well as intellectuals, Ohanjanian played an important role at the Fourth World Congress in Vienna in 1907 and in the Caucasus to put a brake on extreme left- and right-wing dissension, thus helping to preserve the unity of the ARF.

Arrested by the Tsarist police in 1908 during persecutions against revolutionaries, Ohanjanian was sentenced to hard labor in Siberia in 1912 after the infamous Trial of Dashnaktsoutiun. During the trial he had admitted to being a member of the ARF Bureau in order to take the blame upon himself and ensure the release of other ARF members. While in Siberia, he married Roubina, a fellow Armenian revolutionary.

Freed in 1915, he worked to assist Western Armenian refugees. He led a medical group to newly liberated Van to assist the population, and after the evacuation of the Vaspourakan region he continued his medical work in Ejmiatzin, where Western Armenian refugees had settled.

In 1917 and 1918 he was part of the mission sent to Berlin by the Armenian National Council in Tiflis, and then took part in the delegation of the Armenian Republic in Paris led by Avetis Aharonian. He became the third prime minister of Armenia, in May

1920, when the ARF Bureau took over the reins of power to quell Bolshevik uprisings. He resigned as prime minister in November 1920, after the fall of Kars to Turkish forces.

Upon the Sovietization of Armenia, Ohanjanian was arrested but was freed thanks to the February 1921 uprising against the Bolsheviks. He crossed over to Iran and then on to Cairo, Egypt, where he spent the rest of his days as a member of the ARF Bureau and as president of the Hamazkayin cultural and educational association, which he helped found in 1928.

He died in Cairo. He was 74.

*

He was respected… by all segments of the public and comrades, even by members of opposition parties. In both work and personally, he also had close relations with Russian revolutionaries.

With his boundless energy and intensity of idealistic struggle, Hamo particularly came to the fore in the years after the 1905 Russian revolution. As a member of the ARF's Eastern Bureau and a representative of the organization before the public, along with Y[eghishe] Topchian, G[aregin] Khazhak, and others, he was a leading public figure, both in national life and among non-Armenians. And, in particular, he enjoyed prestige among the youth, the militant forces, and workers…. During the time of the [left-wing] "separatists" and [right-wing] "Mihranakans," his role as a moral force was invaluable. With his convictions and personality, Hamo occupied a central place in the Dashnaktsoutiun and was something of a unifying force for both the right and the left.

Simon Vratsian, in Houshapatoum H. H. Dashnaktsoutian: 1890–1950, *Hairenik Press*

PAPKEN SIUNI (BEDROS PARIAN)
1873–1896

PAPKEN SIUNI WAS born in the village of Pingian, in Agn. He graduated from the Ketronakan School in Constantinople. A year before his graduation, he was arrested and jailed briefly for his participation in Armenian protests. After his graduation, he attended the Istanbul Naval Academy and served in the Turkish navy for a year.

Siuni became an adherent of Dashnaktsakan ideology under the guidance of Hovhannes Yousoufian in 1892–1893. Prior to the ARF's establishment in Constantinople, Siuni had organized a group, called "Siunik" (hence his nom de guerre), consisting of students and newcomers from the interior; that group joined the ARF en masse.

Siuni soon became the right hand of Yousoufian and Arshak Vramian. In the newly formed ARF Central Committee of Constantinople, Siuni became the ideological and organizational driving force.

Simultaneously confronting government persecution and the opposition of conservative Armenian circles, including betrayals, he played an integral role in the transfers of arms and ammunition, the preparation of explosives, the teaching and training of recruits, and the day-to-day affairs of the organization.

It was in such a revolutionary environment that Siuni conceived of the seizure of the Ottoman Bank as a response to the Hamidian Massacres of hundreds of thousands of Armenians in the interior. His plan was approved by the Central Committee, and he was entrusted with the leadership and implementation of the operation.

On August 14, 1896, at noon, the time of the planned assault on the bank, only 24 out of the 73 revolutionaries who were to take part in the operation had presented themselves. Conferring with his lieutenants Armen Garo and Hrach Tiriakian, Siuni delayed the attack by an hour. Out of options, at 1 PM he signaled the assault.

The guards posted at the entrance of the bank resisted fiercely. Although they were killed and the assault group was able to enter the bank, Siuni, who was laden with bags filled with grenades and dynamite, was shot as he ascended the stairs to the bank entrance. As a result of the explosion of a grenade in his hand, he was seriously wounded. His comrades were able to bring him into the bank, where he died. He was 23 years old.

The revolutionaries occupied the bank and under the leadership of Armen Garo and Hrach fought off attacking troops until the early hours of August 15.

The operation ended with the safe passage from Constantinople of the remaining 17 revolutionaries, and promises by the European powers that they would pressure the Sultan to refrain from reprisals and end the massacres in the interior of the empire.

*

To the Memory of Papken Siuni (Bank Ottoman)

The Dashnaktsakan Committee
Has seized Bank Ottoman.
In it they have filled
Explosive, destructive bombs.

Every Armenian brave waited
For that dear moment
When the bomb would be thrown
And the enemy would be destroyed.

Behold, from the window fell
A round grenade.

There trembled Sultan Hamid
And his evil Izzet Pasha.

When Hamid heard this news,
He called Nazim to his side.
Go, he said, and pacify
Those restive Armenians.

Bank Ottoman has been placed
Under the command of Papken Siuni.
There, the Dashnaktsakan noble giant,
Papken Siuni, was martyred.

His name terrified
A hundred thousand Muslims
And the one called Sultan Hamid,
The cruel race's caliph.

ALEKSANDR KHATISIAN
1874–1945

KHATISIAN WAS BORN in Tiflis, Georgia, to a well-known Armenian family. His father was a high-ranking official, respected by Armenian and non-Armenian circles alike. His older brother, Konstantin, was a founding member of the ARF.

Khatisian graduated from the Tiflis State Gymnasium (College) and studied medicine at Moscow University and Kharkov University, then went to Germany for specialized studies. He returned to Tiflis and practiced medicine.

He was a person of varied interests, in particular politics and civil service. He was elected to the Tiflis city council in 1902, and by 1906 he was assistant to the mayor of Tiflis. He served as mayor of Tiflis from 1909 to 1917, and from 1914 to 1917 he was president of the association of Caucasus cities (some 44 in number).

He joined Dashnaktsoutiun only after the 1917 Russian Revolution. Though he had wanted to join the party in 1905, he was dissuaded by Rostom, Hamo Ohanjanian, and others; they argued that as a nonpartisan he could better serve the Armenian people and the ARF.

During his political career he was active in civic live, publishing articles, pamphlets on cultural and health-related topics, and translations from Armenian literature. Russian Viceroy Vorontsov-Dashkov consulted with him and prominent civic leader Dr. Hakob Zavriev about the creation of Armenian volunteer units in the summer of 1914.

After the Russian Revolution, when Tiflis came under Georgian rule and the Transcaucasus was de facto separated from Russia, his life took a different tack. He joined the ARF and from 1917 to 1918 he was mayor of Alexandropol (Giumri). He served as a member from the Armenian National Council in Tiflis. After declaration of the independent Republic of Armenia, he served as foreign minister and signed the Treaty of Batum with the Ottoman Empire.

He then served as prime minister from 1919 to 1920. He was sent abroad by the government to secure loans and organize the establishment of the so-called Gold Fund for the republic. Returning to Armenia in time of war, it fell to him to sign the Treaty of Alexandropol in December 1920.

After the Sovietization of Armenia, Khatisian went to Paris and continued his work, including as a representative of Armenian interests at the League of Nations.

He died in Paris, in March 1945. He was 71.

*

On May 28, 1918, at 12 o'clock, the independence of Armenia was declared by the Armenian National Council, in Tiflis.

For days, cannons were roaring on the Plain of Ararat, where the fate of the Armenians was being decided.

Abandoned by the Russian soldiers who rushed back to their homes, and betrayed by its Christian [Georgian] and Muslim [Tatar/Azeri] allies in the Transcaucasus government who were courting with Germany and Turkey, the Armenian people stood as one in those fateful days of May 1918. It rallied around its leaders. The Dashnaktsoutiun dispatched all of its forces to the battlefront.

Inexperienced, unarmed youth, refugees, even women and girls, without regard to class or faction, manned positions alongside the volunteer soldiers who for years had won their laurels on battlefields. All of them heroically confronted the assaults of the enemy's regular armies.

The Republic of Armenia was born of the sacred Armenian blood spilled in abundance on the plain of Ararat.

Finally, the centuries-old dream of Armenians became reality. An independent homeland, on a portion of the historic lands of our forefathers. A preliminary step toward integral, united Armenia.

The Armenian people took in a deep breath of consolation, seeing the name of Armenia recorded—even if in small print—in a corner of the world map.

From a speech delivered on the 20th anniversary of Armenian Independence, in May 1938

ABRAHAM GIULKHANDANIAN
1875–1946

BORN IN VAGHARSHABAD, Ejmiatzin, Giulkhandanian studied at the Gevorgian Seminary and later in Russia at the Yaroslavl Law School. He joined the ARF in 1894, and in 1898 went to Baku on business, remaining there for many years, devoting himself to ARF work.

Giulkhandanian became a member of the ARE Central Committee of Baku in 1902, continuing uninterrupted in that capacity until 1908. During that period, he established close ties between the ARF and Armenian oil well laborers in Baku, earning the respect of Armenians from all classes of society as well as non-Armenians.

An active leader in Baku during the Armeno-Tatar clashes of 1905–1906, he also led the Armenian defense in the Gandzak province (present-day Gyanja, in Azerbaijan).

In 1908, he became a member of the ARF's Eastern Bureau and helped coordinate ARF activities throughout the Caucasus. He was arrested in April 1910, during anti-ARF persecutions headed by government prosecutor Prince Leizhin, and was not freed until 1912. He moved to Yerevan after his release.

In 1914–15, he became a member of the organizing committee of the Armenian Volunteer Movement. In 1918, he returned to Baku, where, with Rostom and other leaders, he helped conduct the heroic defense of the town.

Giulkhandanian served as a member of parliament independent Armenia, later becoming Minister of Justice in Aleksandr Khatisian's cabinet, and subsequently Minister of the Interior. He was also part of Khatisian's delegation that signed the Treaty of Alexandropol with the Bolsheviks in December 1920.

After the Sovietization of Armenia, Giulkhandanian fled to Romania. He eventually settled in Paris as a member of the ARF Bureau, taking charge of organizing the party archives.

An active writer for the rest of his life, Giulkhandanian published numerous books, articles, and memoirs regarding the Caucasus, the Armeno-Tatar conflict, Armenian revolutionary women, and ARF history.

During World War II, he was vice-president of the Armenian National Council in Berlin, and took part in the delegation that negotiated with Germany to form an Armenian regiment in the Caucasus composed of captured Armenian POWs.

He died in France. He was 71.

*

Immediately after the truce [in February, 1905], unprecedented meetings took place in Baku.

It was the first time in the history of the Caucasus that without any permission, without police participation, the people of Baku, irrespective of sect or nationality—Armenian, Jew, Russian, Tatar, and others—gathered together, three to four thousand strong, analyzed the events, criticized the government, and expressed their disgust while protesting the crimes that had been committed.

The meetings took place in the large hall of the citizens' club, as well as in other halls in the oil-producing area of the city. They lasted over two weeks. They served two purposes: (a) to bring out the details of the crimes and to find the criminals; and (b) to expose the base, prevocational role played by the authorities in Baku.

The revolutionary parties of Baku and Russia had never had such an appropriate occasion to disseminate their ideas, and they used this occasion to the utmost. Thousands of citizens gathered together, heard about the unprincipled activities of the government and the inept authorities of Baku, and descriptions of how it had provided weapons to the Tatar murderers. Serious disclosures were being made, especially about Prince Nakashidze, who, during the conflict [between Tatars and Armenians], instead of trying to restore order, had shamelessly and openly encouraged the Tatar criminals.

All the revolutionary parties, which until that moment had operated undercover, in those days lay aside all secrecy and came into the open in the name of their parties, formulated resolutions, and demanded that all those responsible be put on public trial.

The police had totally lost bearings and didn't know what to do. Diminsky, the police chief of the city, immediately after the events of February, had presented his resignation, and a few days later left Baku in haste. Khamitsky, the chief of police of the oil-producing area, as well as his second-in-command, ran away so quickly right after the ceasefire that they did not have time to pass their responsibilities on to their successors. As for the higher-ups, the governor and his aide, they did not dare interfere with the public meetings, perhaps because they felt guilty.

Was it the fourth or the fifth day, that a group of policemen closed the doors of the hall and tried to prevent the public gathering? But the meeting participants were so enraged that in mere seconds they scattered the police, smashed the locked doors, and, invading the hall, began their usual meeting.

The meetings ended with appropriate resolutions that were printed, and thousands of copies were distributed not only in Baku but practically all the cities of Russia, as well as overseas.

From Hay-Tatarakan Endharumnere
(The Armeno-Tatar Clashes), 1933

NIKOL AGHBALIAN
1875–1947

BORN IN TIFLIS, Aghbalian studied at the Nersisian School in his hometown and subsequently Gevorgian College in Ejmiatzin. He later attended universities in Moscow, Paris (the Sorbonne), and Lausanne, Switzerland.

Joining the ranks of the ARF in his youth, he was sent to Egypt in 1905 on organizational work. From 1909 to 1912 he was director of the Armenian National School in Tehran, as well as a member of the ARF Central Committee there.

In 1913 Aghbalian was appointed a member of the *Horizon* editorial team, along with Arshak Jamalian, in Tiflis. He was also a member of the Tiflis National Bureau and the organizing committee of the Armenian Volunteer Movement in 1914–1915.

After Armenian independence, he was elected a member of parliament and appointed Minister of Education. Due to his efforts, the Armenian State University was founded, in Alexandropol, on January 31, 1920.

Aghbalian was arrested by the Bolsheviks on February 9, 1921, but was freed due to the February Revolt 10 days later. He crossed into Iran, then settled in Alexandria, Egypt, where he became director of the Armenian school.

He was a founder of the Hamazkayin Cultural Association in 1928, in Egypt. He also co-founded, together with Levon Shant, Hamazkayin's college (Jemaran) in Beirut, Lebanon, in 1929–1930. He remained in Lebanon as a teacher at the college until his death.

Aghbalian is acknowledged as an erudite philologist and impartial literary critic, gifted with a profound sense of literature and art.

He died in Beirut. He was 74.

*

Dashnaktsoutiun serves the interests of the public and not the interests of its members.... Those who become members of our party must, from the very beginning, be reconciled with an idea that to many may seem askew and meaningless: namely, that he is joining an organization in which he must continually give of himself and sacrifice, without expecting any material gain, and that it is not the party that must sustain him but he who must provide for the party with his work, money, and life.

Thousands of Dashnaktsakans have left home, given up positions and influence, and have entered into an organization that is at once dreadful and attractive; and their only gain has been death. The organization provides its members with invitations for a life of rigor and immolation, not prosperity; in a certain sense, the Dashnaktsoutiun is like the early church. It teaches its members to die for an ideal.... It promises nothing to its members, neither positions, nor honor, nor wealth, nor comfort...

If yesterday you were a simple soldier or squad leader, and today you become a government minister, you do not cease being a Dashnaktsakan who is subject to the [ARF's] Constitution and Bylaws. And if Dashnaktsoutiun notices that in your new position you are attempting to think and work as a non-Dashnaktsakan, it will mercilessly unseat you, without regard to your fame or your position. Many have seen how renowned reputations have been made by the Dashnaktsoutiun for one or another of its members; they have also seen the precipitous fall of the same people, carried out by the same Dashnaktsoutiun: Because Dashnaktsoutiun demands that public affairs be conducted by idealist individuals who serve only the public interest and who dare not, for a minute, consider using their position for personal gain. Thus, various positions toward which glory-seekers madly rush are pure anguish and tribulation for the Dashnaktsakan, for he must reconcile the demands of public office with the candid and humble lifestyle of his calling as an idealist Dashnaktsakan. And it is only through decree that such positions are given to a Dashnaktsakan—not as an honor but as an obligation. To people on the outside all this may seem a legend, but Dashnaktsakans know otherwise.

From the series "Mtatzumner" in Droshak, *1929–30*

VAHAN PAPAZIAN (KOMS)
1876–1973

BORN IN TABRIZ to a family from Van, Koms was the younger brother of writer Vrtanes Papazian. In 1893, he came into contact with revolutionary circles in Nor Nakhijevan "(Rostov-on-Don), and in 1895 he joined the Dashnaktsoutiun in Alexandropol.

In his early years in the party, Koms operated in the Northern Caucasus and Baku. He entered into formal studies, first at Moscow University, later at St. Petersburg University, but did not complete his studies. In St. Petersburg he engaged in revolutionary activities and was forced to flee to Finland when he was implicated in the assassination of a wealthy Armenian. He stayed in Finland as a fugitive for two years, from 1900 to 1902, and thereafter moved to Geneva.

From Geneva, Koms returned secretly to Transcaucasia and then to Van, with Vana Ishkhan, in 1903. There, at the suggestion of Kristapor, he took on the duties of Vardges, the leading fieldworker in the area, who had been imprisoned. A photographer by hobby, he took the only known photo of Kevork Chavoush, on Aghtamar Island, in Van, in 1904.

He remained in Van until 1908, for a time organizing and overseeing the arms and ammunition routes to Western Armenia from Iran and Yerevan. After the restoration of the Ottoman Constitution in 1908, he was elected a member of the Ottoman Parliament from Van.

Koms participated in the ARF Council meeting of September 1912, which, in the wake of Armenian disillusionment with the Young Turks, decided to reactivate and internationalize the Armenian Question. He was in Moush in 1913–1914 to protect the interests of the people there. When the Genocide began, he survived the massacre of 1915 in Moush and with difficulty reached the Caucasus, where he joined the handful of fedayis commanded by Rouben Ter Minasian.

Koms moved on to Tiflis in 1917–18, and in 1919 was elected a member of Armenia's Parliament and appointed a member of the Armenian National Delegation in Paris. He returned to Yerevan later that year to take part in the ARF's Ninth World Congress. He returned to France in September 1920 to take part in further peace talks after the signing of the Treaty of Sevres.

Following the Sovietization of Armenia, in 1921, Koms, along with Vahan Navasardian and Arshak Jamalian, participated in the Riga talks with the Bolsheviks. Those talks, concerning the safety and security of Soviet Armenia and the ARF's position toward it, eventually proved fruitless.

Later, on behalf of the ARF, he worked with the Kurdish liberation movement in Turkey.

In 1947, he settled in Beirut, Lebanon, and became active in the affairs of the Hamazkayin cultural association. He wrote a three-volume work titled *Modest Heroes,* consisting of the biographies of many fedayis; he also published a three-volume memoir.

He died in Beirut. He was 97 years old.

*

Within Alexandropol's youth and students there were a few ardent young men affiliated with the party [ARF] who had gotten in touch with me. In the evenings, they often came to my room, talking arguing, and reading until very late. In this manner the idea sprang forth of organizing a group, and we named the group "Arshalouys" (Dawn). Thereafter, we held periodic meetings, which were devoted to various party matters or to the analysis of current political events. In everyone there was the desire to examine the party's ideology, but at the same time they were not cut off from practical work.

From "From Days Gone By," Hairenik Monthly, *May, 1924*

SIAMANTO (ADOM YARJANIAN)
1878–1915

BORN IN AGN, on the shores of the Euphrates, Yarjanian received his preliminary education in the town's Nersisian School under the guidance of Bishop Karekin Srvantsdiants, who recognized his literary talents and gave him the pen-name Siamanto.

He left for Constantinople in 1892 with his father, who was a merchant, and continued his studies at the Mirijanian School at Kum Kapu and the Berberian School at Scutari (Üsküdar). After the

1895–1896 Hamidian massacres, fleeing the stifling atmosphere in Constantinople, he headed to Greece, then Egypt.

In 1897, Siamanto left for Europe to continue his studies, staying for a time in Geneva, then to Paris, where he studied literature at the Sorbonne for three years. While in Europe, he contributed to *Droshak* and produced some of his best poetry. He published his first volume, *Tiutsaznoren* (Like the Children of Gods), in 1901–02 in Paris. Four more were published during his years in Europe.

In 1909, after the declaration of the Ottoman Constitution of 1908, Siamanto returned to Constantinople, where he wrote for *Azatamart* and published *Garmir Lourer Paregames* (Red News From My Friend).

In December 1909 he was sent to the United States as an ARF fieldworker and to assume the editorship of the *Hairenik* daily. There, in 1910, Siamanto published *Hayreni Hraver* (Invitation From the Homeland), as well as his complete works, which he edited.

In 1911, he returned to Constantinople via London and Paris, and continued his literary and political activities. On the 1500th anniversary of the founding of the Armenian alphabet, in 1913, he published his last volume, *Mesrob Mashtots,* in Constantinople.

The same year, he traveled with the retinue transporting ARF founder Simon Zavarian's casket to Tiflis. He traveled throughout the Transcaucasus, meeting with his Eastern Armenian contemporaries.

He later returned to Constantinople. Arrested in 1915, Siamanto was among the first victims of the Genocide. He was 37 years old.

*

Prayer to Anahid on the Feast of Navasart

Goddess, I purge my conscience of all slothful religions.
And I walk proudly in sacred slippers toward you.
Open the marble gates of your temple. Let me bruise my
forehead on the door.
Open the altar and give back to me the hot strength
of my Artaxian forefathers.

Hear me, golden mother, fertile sister, sister of virtue,
donor of abundance, patroness of Armenians.
Hear me on this morning of the feast of Navasart
when your people rejoice.
Allow me to kneel and pray before your idol.

Listen, miraculous rose, goddess of golden feet,
white bride of nocturnal light, lover of the sun,
nakedness with a body of light, sail of Aramazt,
let the sun burn on your altar again.

I believe in you, as I stand on the hills of Pakrevant.
I, the centuries-old worshipper of God, come armed with a
spear.
I am your son, here as a supplicant apostle,
begging you to hear my lyre of Haig, a lyre born
from the soil of Koght.

I come in the robes of a pilgrim, bearing green
balsam branches and gold rosewater

in a silver pitcher to anoint your breasts.
And here with the rosewater are tears
mourning your destruction.
Deer follow my shadow as I come to you.

Let the pagan life flow again from the hills.
Let tall sons of the sun wear brocade
and arch their bows, planting their spears,
fastening their swords into necks of the bulls
on the threshold of your altars.
Let a white flock of doves fly from the shoulders
of fertile young Armenian brides toward your statue once more.
Let the fountains of Vartavar come to life and flow
and let sixteen-year-old maidens rise to dance
offering their magical bodies to you, goddess of chastity.

Take your revenge now, after twenty centuries,
oh my goddess Anahid, now as I throw
into the fires of your altar, the two poisonous arms
of my cross. And I celebrate you, oh golden mother,
by burning the polluted bone from the rib
of the Illuminator.
I beg of you, oh powerful, unequalled beauty,
give your body to the sun and be fertilized,
give birth to a formidable god for the Armenians.
For us, from your diamond-hard uterus bear an invincible god!

Translation by Diana Der Hovanessian

ARAM MANOUKIAN
(SARGIS HOVHANNISIAN, SERGEY)
1879–1919

BORN IN THE village of Zeyva, in Ghapan, Zangezour, Aram Manoukian attended parochial schools in Shoushi and Yerevan. He joined the ARF at a young age and became an organizer among laborers in Batumi, in 1901, and then in Gandzak and Kars, where by 1903–04 he had already become a highly valued leader.

In 1904 he crossed into Iran, then to Van, where for four years he was the central figure. After the traitor Davo informed Turkish authorities about the location of ARF arms caches, Aram was arrested and tortured. He was eventually released during the Ottoman Constitutional Regime.

He attended the Fourth World Congress in 1907. He was a teacher for a time in Ordu. He then went to Geneva for a year to visit Rouben Ter Minasian, then returned to Van.

In 1915, after Vana Ishkhan and Arshak Vramian were assassinated, Aram was left alone to face a catastrophic situation. He led and became the symbol of the heroic Battle of Van in April 1915, and was appointed governor of free Vaspourakan.

He accompanied the people of Van in their exodus toward the Caucasus. In 1916–17, in Tiflis, Aram was active in the affairs of the ARF Bureau, the Armenian National Council, and Western Armenian refugees.

As the National Council's special envoy and plenipotentiary representative in Yerevan, Aram was proclaimed "dictator" of the Ararat region in May 1918 and led the resistance against the invading Turks. He was the symbol of the victory in the Ararat plain and was considered by the population as the founder of the Armenian Republic.

In the Republic's first government (under Hovhannes Kachaznouni as prime minister), Aram was Minister of the Interior and Minister of Supplies. He contracted typhus, which was wreaking havoc at that time, and died at age 40, on January 29, 1919.

*

But why do we consider the comfort and happiness built by Europe upon our misfortunes as humanitarianism?... Oh, how I wish for the day when the orphanages and all such similar bourgeois institutions will cease to serve as "oases" for our people, when the people of this unfortunate nation will be able to—with the genius of its own culture and its own just economic merits—establish, for all of the country and all of its masses and peoples, an oasis more diverse and fundamental…

From Aram Manoukian's Memoirs

ROUBEN TER MINASIAN (MINAS TER MINASIAN)
1882–1951

BORN IN AKHALKALAK (present-day Georgia) to parents who had migrated from Erzurum, Rouben studied at the Gevorgian Seminary in Ejmiatzin and then at the Lazarian College in Moscow. He then served as an officer in the Russian army.

As a young ARF organizer, he was molded into a Dashnaktsakan in the intense revolutionary activity of the "Kars Furnace" in 1903–04. He was dispatched to Van in 1905 as a plenipotentiary representative of the ARF.

He joined Aram Manoukian in Van, then operated in the Lernabar region (south of Lake Van), but after tactical differences with Vana Ishkhan he left for Sasoun to back up Kevork Chavoush in 1906. He stayed there until the proclamation of the Ottoman Constitution, having taken sole charge of the Dashnaktsakan fedayi forces in Sasoun after the death of Kevork Chavoush in May 1907.

He attended the Fifth ARF World Congress, in Varna, Bulgaria, in 1909 and then left for Geneva to resume his studies. Summoned to Moush in 1913, he later went to Sasoun and with his veteran fedayis led the heroic defense of Sasoun against regular Turkish forces and Kurdish irregulars in 1915. With a handful of men he broke through enemy lines and crossed into the Caucasus.

In 1917–18, he was a member of the Armenian National Council, based in Tiflis, and was elected to the parliament of Independent Armenia. He was elected to the ARF Bureau at the Ninth World Congress in Yerevan and remained a member of it virtually without interruption until his death.

He served as minister of war in the Bureau-government of Ohanjanian, playing a leading role in suppression of Bolshevik riots and the elimination of Turko-Tatar insurrections in Armenia.

After the Sovietization of Armenia, he went to Zangezour, then crossed into Iran, and eventually traveled to France, Egypt, and Lebanon, and finally settled in Paris.

The seven volumes of Rouben's memoirs, *Memoirs of an Armenian Revolutionary,* are exceptionally valuable both as testimonies about men and events and as a storehouse of revolutionary ideas and analyses.

He died in Paris on November 29, 1950, at the age of 69.

*

At sunset the fedayis would rise to their feet, regardless of the darkness and the inclemency of the weather. Like the wolves they had to prefer the dark night. At such times the fedayi is more formidable to the enemy. The fedayi loves to travel on rainy or snowy nights.

When the fedayi is ready to take off, he embraces and kisses his comrades, they crack jokes, and the entire community's men, women, and children bid them farewell with tearful eyes. The word used on such occasions is "Oughour," which means "God be with you [good luck]." The fedayis respond by saying, "Shen Mnak," which means, "May you be prosperous [be well]." Generally the villagers are forbidden to accompany the fedayis. On frequent occasions they appoint a villager to stand guard so that no one shall see in what direction the fedayis move.

After they leave the village, the fedayis themselves do not know where they are going. They stop at the outskirts of the village, waiting for the orders of the company commander, who alone known where they are going. The latter calls two fedayis who are his best scouts and whispers in their ear the direction he wants to take. The scouts instantly take their place at the head of the company, make a detour, and circle the whole village to confuse the villagers. The company follows the scouts at a distance of 50 to 100 paces, the company commander marching on their side or in the rear, always accompanied by two aides. The company follows the commander at a distance of ten paces. Two fedayis lag behind to act as rear guards.

On the march it is strictly forbidden to talk to one another; likewise, smoking or coughing are out. The rifles are sheathed with a cloth jacket to prevent glinting in the sunshine, or grating against the bandoliers or rocks. The careless fedayi is promptly brought back to his senses by the corporal's or company commander's solid fist on the nape of his neck, and the company resumes the trail…

The fedayis are good marchers, easily making a distance of 5 to 6 kilometers in one hour. Each night they cover a distance of 25 to 40 kilometers, the idea being the longer distance they leave behind, the better. They generally shun the villages on the road to prevent detection. They cross the rivers and streams with great care, never removing their clothes, in order to gain time. The bandolier is never taken off, even though at times the baggy trouser is shed. It is too risky to be separated from one's weapons even for a moment.

After a march of three to four hours the fedayi is permitted to smoke a cigarette, provided he is careful to hide the light of his match. The night march must come to its end by daybreak when the company has reached its destination. Upon arrival the company does not enter the place at once but halts some distance away until the scouting is completed. Two fedayis enter the village and call at the home of the most reliable person. They explain the purpose of their call, and after taking stock of the situation, they return to the camp, accompanied by a villager who leads the company to their quarters, generally four to five homes best suited against surprise attack.

In the morning, when the village comes to life, no one knows about the visitors except the host families. By afternoon the word spreads and in the evening preparations are made for a public meeting and the order of business.

The fedayi does not rest immediately upon his arrival, but

first is feted by the hosts. Then he retires into a dark corner of the stable or the barn. At daybreak one of them stands guard while the rest go to sleep on blankets, their rifles carefully tucked between their legs. It is strictly forbidden to take off the bandolier. Thus taking turns, they sleep into the afternoon.

From Memoirs of an Armenian Freedom Fighter, *1963, Hairenik Press, James G. Mandalian, translator*

SIMON VRATSIAN (SIMON GROUZINIAN)
1882–1969

BORN IN THE village of Metz Sala in Nor Nakhijevan, in the Northern Caucasus, Vratsian received his education at the Gevorgian Seminary in Ejmiatzin. He joined the ARF in 1898, mistakenly believing he was joining the Hnchaks: He had entered the wrong room in a building where both the Hnchaks and the Dashnaks were holding meetings.

He returned to Nor Nakhijevan as a Dashnak fieldworker and represented the region at the ARF's Fourth World Congress in

Vienna in 1907. At that meeting, he supported the party's adoption of socialism as a principal plank in its platform.

In 1908, Vratsian attended the University of St. Petersburg to study law and education. In 1910, after stays in Moscow, Constantinople, and Batumi, he settled for a time in Erzurum. There, he taught at a local school and edited a local newspaper, and was briefly jailed under suspicion of being a Russian spy.

In 1911, he went to America, where he became editor of the *Hairenik* daily newspaper. Three years later, he represented the party's American organization at the ARF's Eighth World Congress (1914) in Erzurum, playing a key role in discussions regarding party policy vis-à-vis the Young Turk leadership. He was elected a member of the ARF's Bureau of Armenia.

He then went to the Caucasus and became a member of the committee organizing the Armenian Volunteer Movement. After the disbandment of the Armenian units, he worked as editor of *Horizon,* in Tiflis, in 1917.

An important figure in the Independent Republic of Armenia (1918–1920), Vratsian was elected to the parliament in 1918 and later served as minister of labor and agriculture in the Ohanjanian cabinet (May to November, 1920). He helped organize the ARF's 9th World Congress in 1919 in Yerevan, where he was elected to the party's Bureau. Thereafter, he was elected a member of the ARF Bureau several times.

In the fall of 1920, immediately after the Armeno-Turkish War, he was appointed prime minister. As such, it was his task, on December 2, 1920, to transfer power officially to the Bolshevik Revolutionary Committee (Revkom).

During the February 1921 popular uprising, Vratsian was

president of the Committee for the Salvation of the Fatherland. Upon expelling the Bolsheviks, he appealed for assistance to Europe, America, and finally to Kemalist Turkey as well. In April, as Soviet troops invaded Armenia, he escaped with thousands of Armenians to Iran. From there, he went to Bombay, Alexandria, and Constantinople, and eventually Paris.

From 1925 to 1933 he worked on *Droshak* (which had been moved to Paris) with Arshak Jamalian and Shavarsh Missakian. He then published the periodical *Vem* and his main work, *The Republic of Armenia*.

A world traveler, Vratsian went to South America in 1936, North America in 1939, and many other places until finally settling in Lebanon. In 1945, he presented a petition at the founding conference of the United Nations, in San Francisco, demanding the return of Turkish-occupied territories to Armenia.

In 1952, after the death of Levon Shant, he became principal of the Hamazkayin Jemaran, in Beirut, and wrote seven volumes of memoirs and other works. He remained at the Jemaran until his death, in 1969, at age 87.

*

And the people of the Plain of Ararat stand up as one....

General Silikian, through a series of orders and appeals, puts the army into order and enhances its military might. Everyone is busy with rear-echelon activities. The women and girls prepare food, tobacco, bandages. The clergy go out among the people and army, cross in hand, and preach sermons. The historic days of Vardanants are being repeated.

When on May 21 the Turks, moving by train, appeared near

Sardarabad, they found before them Armenian soldiers emboldened by the determination to triumph. General Silikian's forces in those days reached approximately 10,000 men. Those forces were divided into two sections: one under the command of Dro, on the Bash Abaran front, the other under the command of Daniel Beg Piroumian, at Sardarabad. The commander-in-chief was General Silikian; the chief of staff was Colonel Vekilian, who had drawn up the general battle plan.... The entire country, become as one man, one soul, was fighting against its mortal enemy.

On May 24, the Turks turned and fled.

From Hayastani Hanrapetutiun, *Beirut, 1958*

REUBEN DARBINIAN
(ARTASHES CHILINGIRIAN)
1883–1968

BORN IN AKHALKALAK, Darbinian was taken to Ekaterinodar (present-day Krasnodar) as a child by his parents. He was educated there and in Tiflis. In 1903 he attended Moscow University, and later traveled to Germany to further his studies.

He joined the ARF in the early 1900s, and by 1906 he had become chairperson of its North Caucasus Central Committee. Due to his revolutionary activities, he was forced by Tsarist authorities to flee in 1909.

Moving to Constantinople, Darbinian continued his activities, becoming editor of the ARF organ *Azatamart*. In 1914, he returned to Tiflis, and from there went on to Baku as editor of various ARF papers.

During the "Baku Commune" of 1918, Darbinian traveled to Moscow with Simon Hakobian to secure Bolshevik aid against the Turkish forces besieging Baku. In Moscow, however, he was met with hostility on the part of Soviet authorities.

In 1919, Darbinian moved on to Yerevan, where he became Minister of Justice in the government of Aleksandr Khatisian. He also served for a time as editor of the party organ *Harach*.

When the Bolsheviks occupied Armenia in late 1920, Darbinian attempted to flee but was apprehended and jailed. He was freed by the popular revolt of February 1921, and during the ensuing months he remained in Armenia as editor of *Azat Hayastan*. He escaped the return of the Bolsheviks by going to Tabriz (Iran) and from there to the West.

Darbinian eventually settled in Boston, where he assumed editorship of *Hairenik* in March 1922. During his long tenure, Darbinian became known for cultivating the talents of many writers and cultural figures, and he oversaw the founding and enlargement of publications that served to supplement the *Hairenik* daily: the English-language *Hairenik Weekly*, the scholarly and literary *Armenian Review*, and the *Hairenik Monthly*, which was notable for publishing the memoirs of many early Dashnak leaders.

Darbinian was also known for his strong, uncompromising anti-Communist stance—a view he held throughout his middle and later years.

He died in Boston. He was 85.

When, after a three-month illness I once again stepped onto the streets of Moscow [1919], I was truly terrified. It seemed the entire city had been subjected to a terrible pogrom. All the shops were closed. Their shelves were emptied. Sometimes only a few pieces of cardboard, leftover goods, and piles of dirt were the only remnants of a once-plentiful, prosperous store. The shattered furniture and windows left no doubt that the hands of vandals had been the cause of this wholesale destruction.

I was sick abed when I read the Soviet decrees about the nationalization of business. I never dreamed that these decrees could in reality have wrought such havoc; to complete the picture, the Bolsheviks had removed all signs and marquees of the stores, without which the city looked completely transfigured and desolate…

Not only in the evenings or at night were the streets empty, but even in the daytime, with the exception of those hours when government clerks or the workers were on their way to, or returning from, their work. After 4 PM (which in reality was 1 PM, because the Bolsheviks, by a crazy whim, had advanced the clock three hours), all the streets of Moscow were empty. Only at times casual passersby stalked the streets like ghosts. Only one thing was stamped on all faces: Terror! All seemed to be fleeing from something, all were in haste, almost running. Men or women were seen, carrying on their shoulders or sometimes on small carts, loaded bags or packages filled with flour, bread, potatoes, or blocks of wood for fuel. It seemed men had no other occupation but to seek something to eat or burn.

Only after long weeks did the Soviet government open a few stores, where, according to public announcement, goods could be procured with special rationing cards. These cards were of four classes: (1) The workers, the most privileged class, whose allowance was more than all other classes'; (2) ranking Soviet functionaries; (3) the non-ranking public servants; and last, (4) all the remainder, namely, the bourgeoisie and the nobility. With the merging of the first two classes, however, soon the public was divided into three classes. In other words, these very same Bolsheviks who were loudest in their condemnation of the classes, now created new classes even on a simple matter as the dispensation of life's necessities.

From "A Mission to Moscow," Memoirs of Reuben Darbinian, 1948, the Armenian Review, *Vol. 1*

VAHAN CARDASHIAN
1883–1934

B ORN IN CAESAREA (Kayseri), in Armenia Minor, Vahan Cardashian was of middleclass parentage. He arrived in the United States in 1902, knowing little English but determined to make a living.

Soon after his arrival in 1902, Cardashian met and married a wealthy American widow who was a prominent women's rights activist. (They divorced in 1916.) With her help, he gained admittance to Yale University Law School in 1904 and worked his way through school.

Cardashian quickly became an excellent writer and during his law school years displayed signs of things to come with his book *The Ottoman Empire of the Twentieth Century* and his article "A Brief Commentary on the Eastern Question," both strongly anti-imperialist in content.

After law school, Cardashian moved to New York City, where he opened a private law practice. During World War I, he left his practice to become Secretary at the Ottoman Embassy in Washington, in 1911. In that capacity, he represented the Ottoman government at various functions and met prominent public figures with whom he developed lasting friendships.

The turning point in Cardashian's career came in 1915, when news of the Armenian massacres reached his ears. He quickly became disillusioned with the Turkish government, submitting scathing criticisms to his superiors, as a result of which he was fired. Thereafter, Cardashian became a sworn enemy of the Turkish government and a ceaseless supporter of the Armenian Cause.

Using his own personal resources and connections, Cardashian opened an Armenian Press Bureau in 1918, intended to educate American public opinion and high official circles about the Armenian Question. In his capacity as director of the Press Bureau, Cardashian authored numerous letters and newspaper articles, sending them to hundreds of groups and persons who could play a role in shaping American policy toward Armenia. A persuasive speaker, Cardashian also spent considerable time lecturing to Armenian and non-Armenian gatherings about the Armenian Cause.

Soon after the creation of the Armenian Press Bureau,

Cardashian felt it imperative to form a larger structure around it. That structure eventually became the American Committee for the Independence of Armenia (ACIA), composed of prominent Americans and university-educated Armenian-Americans who worked as volunteers, often lending their names to efforts that Cardashian himself would orchestrate.

Prominent ACIA board members included former Secretary of State Elihu Root, Near East Relief Chairman Cleveland Dodge, and Senator Henry Cabot Lodge (who, ironically, would later oppose a US mandate for independent Armenia because of political ambitions).

The ACIA existed from 1918 until 1927. Cardashian guided its efforts in a determined yet flexible manner, varying his tactics in accordance with Armenia's ever-changing geopolitical position.

Although he never joined the ARF, Cardashian worked very closely with the party leadership and received considerable funding from the ARF to carry out the ACIA's work. He developed a particularly close relationship with ARF leader Dr. Garegin Pastermajian (Armen Garo), Independent Armenia's Ambassador to Washington.

After the disbandment of the ACIA in 1927, Cardashian continued to work tirelessly as an individual, submitting papers, memoranda, etc., and investing most of his personal funds into the effort to publicize the Armenian Cause.

Cardashian died a pauper in 1934, and the ARF solicited funds from the community to pay for his funeral. At the time of his death, Cardashian was the lead defense lawyer for the seven men put to trial for the 1933 assassination of Archbishop Ghevont (Leon) Tourian in New York City.

*

Force—actual or potential—is the initial basis of government. Rarely in history has an independent State ever been set up except by force, and by a demonstrated ability to use force.

Inadequate force—or misdirected force—is a waste, and often results in great, perhaps lasting, damage.

Force—particularly, collective force—should never be resorted to except (a) when all other processes have failed to preserve a vital right; (b) as a reprisal against governmental terrorism and lawlessness, and (c) as a demonstration of will and power to defend a vital right.

Threat is ordinarily a confession of weakness. Threat by one who is reputed or regarded as being powerless, is an empty gesture, and is harmful.

Force alone can achieve independence, but it alone cannot keep it. Sound leadership, good diplomacy and economic independence, plus force, retain political independence. Geographical position and change in international alignments determine, prolong, or shorten the life of a State which possesses force, but which is, otherwise, lacking in the essential element to the maintenance of an independent State.

From "Force and Diplomacy," Armenian Review,
Vol. 22, Number 1 (Spring 1969)

DRO (DRASTAMAT KANAYAN)
1884–1956

BORN IN SURMALU (present-day Igdir, Turkey), in the Yerevan governerate of the Russian Empire, Dro was one of the most daring avengers and military figures of Dashnaktsoutiun. He attended the local parish school, then a Russian high school in Yerevan.

He joined the ARF in 1903, during Russian attempts to confiscate Armenian Church properties—a move that the ARF actively opposed.

Dro was tasked by the ARF Central Committee of Baku to punish those responsible for inciting the Tatar (Azeri) mobs and touching off the Armeno-Tatar confrontations in 1905. Georgian noble Prince Nakashidze, who had been vice-governor of Yerevan and participated in the seizures of Armenian Church properties, was appointed governor of Baku in 1904 and encouraged Tatar atrocities against the Armenians of the city. In May 1905, Dro assassinated Nakashidze in Baku.

Later, in 1907 in Alexandropol, he and Martiros Charoukhchian assassinated General Alikhanov, who had been in Nakhijevan in 1905 during Tatar attacks against Armenians and later led a Cossack division in Armenia. In 1908, Dro settled in Bayazit, in the guise of a merchant, to supervise arms shipments.

In 1915 Dro commanded the Second Armenian Volunteer Regiment. Later, he played a vital role in the decisive battles of 1918, gaining the victory at Bash Abaran, which, along with the victories at Sardarabad and Gharakilise, paved the way for the founding of the Armenian Republic of 1918.

Dro was a general in the armed forces of the Armenian Republic and served as minister of war in the Vratsian cabinet. After the Sovietization of Armenia, he was exiled to Moscow, then made his way to Romania.

During the Second World War, his efforts to protect Armenians in areas under German occupation, as well as Armenian prisoners of war in Nazi camps, helped save thousands of Armenian lives.

Dro settled in Lebanon in 1947. He died in Boston, in 1956, at the age of 73.

His remains were taken to Armenia for final burial in Aparan

(Bash Abaran), on May 28, 2000, as part of the commemoration of the 82nd anniversary of the First Republic of Armenia.

*

Death would have been unavoidable had it not been for the dedication of his comrades-in-arms. The command of the regiment passed on to Armen Garo. The wounded Dro was taken to Igdir, suffering unspeakable difficulties and torment, and from there to Tiflis, to the Aramian hospital, where he underwent surgery and treatment. But the bullet stayed in his lungs, accompanying him for the rest of his life…. It was during those days [the Russo-Turkish War], in the beginning of December, that Tsar Nicholas came to Tiflis. He also visited the military hospitals. Escorted by Mayor [Aleksandr] Khatisian and doctors and nurses, he entered the room in which Dro lay.

Khatisian informed the Tsar about Dro's person and the circumstances of his being wounded. The Tsar, delighted, congratulated Dro, and bestowing him with the cross of bravery, asked: "Where did you learn the military arts?"

"In revolution, your highness," Dro answered without hesitation.

In revolution, in Russian—"v revoluzii"—has greater impact. The Tsar, a mean-spirited man who was fearful by nature and hated revolutionaries, was taken aback and wanted to leave. Khatisian rushed to calm him, stating that the comment referred to the revolution of the Armenians in Turkey… The next morning all of Tiflis was speaking with awe about the meeting between Dro and the Tsar.

Simon Vratsian, in Kianki Ughinerov, Vol. 4.

SCHAVARCH MISSAKIAN
(SHAVARSH MISAKIAN)
1884–1957

BORN IN THE village of Zonar, in Sepasdia (Sivas), Missakian studied at the Ketronakan Armenian School of Constantinople. He started working as a journalist at 16, first as editor of *Sourhandak* (messenger), and later, during the Hamidian regime, as a publisher and distributor of revolutionary literature.

In 1908, after the proclamation of the Ottoman Constitution, he published a literary paper, *Azdak* (Factor), in collaboration with noted literary figures Zabel Yesayan, Kegham Parseghian, and Vahram Tatoul.

In 1911, he moved to Garin (Erzurum), where he stayed for a year as editor of *Harach* in place of the assassinated Yeghishe Topjian, and toured the Moush and Sasoun regions with an armed squad headed by Rostom.

Upon returning to Constantinople, he joined the editorial staff of *Azatamart*. During the deportations and massacres of April 1915, Missakian managed to escape the mass arrests and lived in hiding in the precinct of Pera for one year. During that period he collected important documents on the Turkish deportations and smuggled them abroad. Unable to find Missakian, the government arrested his father and exiled him to Konya (he later escaped).

In 1916, Missakian tried to move to Bulgaria from Istanbul but was betrayed by a Bulgarian who served as a spy for Turkey. Arrested in March, Missakian was imprisoned, interrogated, and tortured for several months, after which he attempted to commit suicide. His death sentence was later commuted to five years' imprisonment. He was eventually freed upon the Allied occupation of Constantinople in November 1918.

After the armistice, Missakian became editor-in-chief of *Chakatamart* (Battle) in Constantinople. In 1919, he took part in the Ninth ARF World Congress in Yerevan. He was elected to the Armenian Parliament. He went to Sofia in 1922, and then to Paris, where he founded the *Haratch* newspaper, first as a tri-weekly and eventually as a daily.

He was elected to the ARF Bureau at the Tenth World Congress in Paris, in 1925 and served on that body until 1933. During those eight years, he also published *Droshak* with Simon Vratsian and Arshak Jamalian.

During his tenure at *Haratch,* Missakian became respected for his wide-ranging knowledge and clarity of vision, perhaps becoming best known for his daily column "Mer Khoske" (Our Word). His output was vast and beneficial, in France especially, for the ARF and for the Armenian community in general.

He was also active in Armenian literary circles as a poet, critic, and translator. During the Nazi occupation of France, forced to discontinue the publication of his paper, he devoted his time to the publication of several literary anthologies under the titles *Haygashen* and *Aradzani*. Upon the restoration of normal conditions following World War II, he resumed the publication of *Haratch* as a daily newspaper.

Missakian died in Paris, in 1957.

*

Our language, our literature, our young generation are being disfigured, together with our mores. Our community in the dispersion is losing its character. What miracles could be wrought by our talented writers in Armenia, if only they were free? In Armenia there is voluntary or involuntary ignorance, confusion of minds, and tension of the nerves. In the Dispersion, the extollers of Stalin have become "talented poets." Our clergymen have become cunning and have deserted our faith, the faith of Christ; they have abandoned their calling. The adventurers have thrived. Our papers are full of charlatanry and dishonest controversies. An era of cheap patriotism has come into being, without the spirit of sacrifice.

All these are bad signs, portending the decline of the race. When are we ever going to recover our soul? Whither are we going? *Quo vadis,* O Armenian people!

From Haratch *[France], ca. 1940*

GAREGIN NZHDEH
(GAREGIN TER HAROUTIUNIAN)
1886–1955

NZHDEH WAS BORN in the village of Kznout, in Nakhijevan, the youngest of four children. His father was the village priest. Nzhdeh received his early education at a Russian school in the city of Nakhijevan. He continued his education at the Tiflis Russian Gymnasium (high school), then attended St. Petersburg University. After two years of study at the Faculty of Law there, he returned to the Caucasus to join the Armenian national liberation movement against the Russian and the Ottoman Empires.

In 1906, Dashnaktsoutiun sent Nzhdeh to Bulgaria to attend military school. He graduated from the Sofia military academy in 1907. In 1908, he participated in the Iranian constitutional revolution alongside Rostom, Yeprem Khan, Mourad of Sepasdia, and other Armenian revolutionaries.

In 1909, Nzhdeh was arrested in the Caucasus by the Russian authorities and spent three years in prison but eventually managed to escape. In 1912, he joined Antranig's Armenian battalion within the Macedonian-Adrianopolitan Volunteer Corps of the Bulgarian Army and fought against the Ottoman Empire in the Balkan wars, during which he was wounded.

Nzhdeh returned to the Caucasus in 1914–1915 to help in the formation of the Armenian volunteer regiments within the Russian army to fight against the Ottoman Empire. He was second in command to Dro, who commanded the Second Armenian Regiment. In 1916, Nzhdeh commanded a special Armenian-Yezidi military unit.

Nzhdeh played a key role in organizing the troops for the defense of Gharakilise in May 1918. After the declaration of the independent First Republic of Armenia, Nzhdeh was appointed governor of Nakhijevan. In August 1919, he was appointed commander of the Southern Corps of the Armenian army.

Following the Sovietization of Armenia in December 1920, the Bolsheviks proposed that Karabagh and Zangezour be granted to Soviet Azerbaijan. Nzhdeh, who vehemently opposed the idea, led the defense of Siunik region against the rising Bolshevik movement and declared Siunik's autonomy.

After the February 1921 revolt against Soviet rule in Yerevan, the ARF controlled Yerevan and surrounding regions for some 42 days before being overwhelmed by numerically superior Red Army troops in April. The leaders of the rebellion then retreated into the Siunik region.

In April 1921, the independence of the self-governing region of Zangezour and surrounding areas was declared the Republic of Mountainous Armenia (Lernahayastani Hanrapetoutiun). Nzhdeh was proclaimed its prime minister and minister of defense.

After months of fierce battles with the Red Army, the Republic of Mountainous Armenia capitulated in July 1921, following Soviet Russia's promises to keep the mountainous region a part of Armenia. Nzhdeh, his soldiers, and Armenian intellectuals, including leaders of the first Independent Republic of Armenia, crossed the Arax River into neighboring Iran. Soon thereafter, Nzhdeh returned to Sofia, Bulgaria, where he married a local Armenian woman and started a family.

Nzhdeh was involved in organizing the Armenian communities of Bulgaria, Romania, and the United States. In 1933, by decision of the ARF, Nzhdeh moved to the US to organize the youth. Assisted by Kopernik Tandourjian, Nzhdeh founded the Tseghagron movement, which soon became the Armenian Youth Federation (the ARF's youth organization.)

In 1937, he returned to Bulgaria, where he published the *Razmik* Armenian newspaper and, along with a group of Armenian intellectuals in Sofia, founded the Taron Nationalist Movement and published its organ, the *Taroni Artziv* paper. He maintained close contacts with Macedonian Bulgarian revolutionary organizations.

During the Second World War, Nzhdeh attempted to gain the support of the Axis Powers (namely, Germany) as well as the Allied Powers (specifically, the Soviet Union) by proposing Armenian assistance in return for attacking Turkey. Convinced to travel to Moscow for talks, he was arrested and held in Lubyanka prison.

In November 1946, Nzhdeh was sent to Yerevan for trial, and on April 24, 1948, he was sentenced to 25 years' imprisonment. Between 1948 and 1952, Nzhdeh was kept in the Vladimir prison for dangerous criminals, in Vladimir, Russia, about 100 miles northeast of Moscow. He was then transferred to Yerevan and kept in a secret prison there until the summer of 1953, and was subsequently returned to Vladimir.

According to fellow prisoner Hovhannes Devejian, Nzhdeh's transfer to Yerevan was related to an attempt to mediate between the Dashnaktsoutiun and the Soviet leadership. After long negotiations with the security services of Soviet Armenia, Nzhdeh and Devejian prepared a letter in Yerevan prison (1953) addressed to ARF leader Simon Vratsian, calling for co-operation with the Soviets regarding the issue of the Armenian struggle against Turkey. However, the Communist Party leadership in Moscow rejected the undertaking.

Receiving a telegram from the Soviet authorities announcing Nzhdeh's death in 1955, his brother, Levon Ter Haroutiunian, left Yerevan for Vladimir. He received Nzhdeh's watch and clothing but was not allowed to take Nzhdeh's writings. The authorities also did not allow the transfer of Nzhdeh's body to Armenia. Nzhdeh was buried in Vladimir.

On August 31, 1983, his remains were secretly transferred from Vladimir to Soviet Armenia as a result of the direct efforts of Pavel Ananian, the husband of Nzhdeh's granddaughter, with the help of Varag Arakelian, Gourgen Armaghanian, Garegin Mkhitarian, Artsakh Buniatian, and Zhora Barseghian.

On April 26, 2005, during the celebration of the 84th anniversary of the Republic of Mountainous Armenia, parts of Nzhdeh's remains were reburied on the slopes of Mount Khoustoup, near Kapan, in Siunik, per Nzhdeh's wishes.

*

There's nothing odd about it: We were massacred, and abandoned [by Europe], because we were completely unfamiliar with the psychology of the European.

We had Christian feelings toward Europe, and because of our abnormal mysticism—our national pathology—we projected our own frame of mind unto the Europeans and therefore deeply believed that all Christian nations felt about us what we felt about them, and that all their battles were being waged for the sake of our salvation.

That self-deception led us to a politics of begging, and because we were also weak, we gave ourselves over to maudlin sentimentality.... Today we curse those political patrons, but we forget that beggars…are given poorhouses, not independent homelands.

We were thus yesterday, when we were a religious flock; today, we have pretensions of being a political force, but we haven't liberated ourselves from the flock psychology, which has penetrated the mentality of our political movements; as a result, they have subconsciously clung to the concept of *orientation*.

True, a noticeable step forward—from Christian superstition to a policy of orientation—but in all that there is an admission: that certain elements of our people are not yet ready for politics, that they are immature, impotent, and timorous, therefore not completely liberated from the previous mentality.

In the meanderings of Armenian political thought, this is a second phase—the phase of semi-independent thought.... This phase has already had disastrous consequences in a short time, and it seems to be continuing to darken and to bloody our prospects even more by internally dividing and weakening our people.

Those currents have already manifested themselves as political groupings that have Russian or Western—there is even talk of Turkish—orientations. Their mindless and… pointless clashes greatly facilitated the fall of Armenia and its division between Turkey and Russia.

However, the consequences of this mentality are not merely political losses.

What's most terrifying is that it will constantly impart to our people the conviction that it is weak and in need of the patronage of others, thus destroying its will and weakening it—rendering it incapable of organizing even its self-defense with its own forces.

Those nations that aspire for independence must first rid themselves of that mentality.…

Tomorrow we will be lost forever if we retain that mentality. We will find salvation if we rid ourselves of preconceptions, if we attempt to stand up—not because of external prompts, at foreigners' behest, but because of our internal, natural, uninhibited drive.

That is how any nation is liberated and becomes free.

If on that path auxiliary forces are to be found, then we will utilize them as allies, as supporters.

Utilize, not entreat: If Armenians understand the difference… then they are on the right path.

From the booklet Open Letters to the Armenian Intelligentsia, *Beirut, 1929.*

VAHAN NAVASARDIAN
1886–1956

BORN IN SHOUSHI, Karabagh, Vahan Navasardian received his early education in his hometown. Thereafter, he went to Baku, where he received a Russian secondary education. He then traveled to Russia, where he received hia higher education at St. Petersburg University, earning a doctorate in history and economics. Self-taught in Armenian, he overcame that seeming handicap and became an excellent writer in a variety of genres in Armenian (journalism, essays, historical abstracts, etc.).

He joined the ARF as a young man and until 1921 worked in various capacities throughout Russia and Eastern Armenia. At the age of 19, he was elected a member of the ARF Central Committee of Baku, performing both public and internal organizational functions. For a brief period, during World War I, he taught Russian, politics, and economics at the Gevorgian Seminary, at Ejmiatzin.

In 1917, he briefly became the mayor of Alexandropol. In May 1918, he participated in the fighting at Gharakilise. Later that year, he became editor of *Horizon*, in Tiflis. He settled in Yerevan in 1919 and became a member of parliament and editor of the ARF organ *Harach*.

In 1920, Navasardian fought in the Armeno-Kemalist war of September-November. Forced underground by the subsequent Sovietization of Armenia, he was active in organizing the February 1921 revolt. The brutal period of Sovietization and the ensuing Armenian struggles against Bolshevik tyranny left an indelible mark on Navasardian, who thereafter became a staunch opponent of Communism.

After the Sovietization of Armenia, he eventually settled in Egypt, after stops in Istanbul and Berlin, and served as editor of *Houssaper* in Cairo. The paper flourished under his tenure, shifting from a semi-weekly to a daily and attracting many of the most prominent Armenian writers and cultural figures in the Middle East.

For many years, Navasardian was a leading member of the ARF, taking an uncompromising stance toward the Soviet regime and its supporters.

An author of prolific and diverse output, he is well known for his books *Bolshevizme yev Dashnaktsoutiune* (Bolshevism and the ARF) and *H. H. Dashnaktsoutian Gaghaparabanoutiune* (The Ideology of the A. R. Federation).

*

Yesterday, the likes of Dreyfus, Farrar, and Beylis… and the powerful voices of great liberals reverberated from continent to continent.

"J'accuse," Emile Zola thundered during the Dreyfus Affair.

"A matter of a way of life," under this simple title, a great Russian, Vladimir Korolenko, was mobilizing the conscience of Russia against the abnormalities of the Tsarist regime.

"Red Sultan," roared from the Thames that other lion of liberalism, Gladstone, against Hamid.

"I can't remain silent," declared Lev Tolstoy, in his powerful voice, on the occasion of the Tsarist mass hangings, thus raising the conscience of the world against the Tsars.

And thus were many others on the five continents of our world.

And these attacks against Tyranny and Evil did not remain without echo.

There was fire in the words of Zola, Tolstoy, Gladstone, and Korolenko; there was a contagious passion for Ideal, Conviction, and Principle, which through understandable channels was being transferred from country to country and through the masses, creating a tempest in souls, pitting liberty against tyranny, and raising enthusiastic multitudes in defense of liberty.

Today, all of them are silent; even those who have assumed the mantle of "liberalism" not only do not protest against the unspeakable tyranny and crimes which are being committed in the huge

Soviet world, but they even possess a hidden sympathy in their hearts toward those who are committing these crimes. Not one protest. Not one occasion. Not one voice of rebellion, powerful, contagious… from anywhere.

From "The Creed of Liberty," Hairenik Monthly, *June 1951*

GARO SASSOUNI
1889–1977

GARO SASSOUNI WAS born in the Aharonk village of Sasoun. He attended the Mkhitarist intermediate school of Moush in 1904–1906, and joined a youth group of the Dashnaktsoutiun in 1904. He taught in Diyarbekir from 1906 to1909.

He studied law in Constantinople in 1909. Three years later, he was sent by the ARF's Western Bureau to Moush and Sasoun. Returning to law school, he graduated in 1914. For the next five years he served in various capacities to prepare the defense of the population in Eastern Armenia.

In October 1914, he went to Transcaucasia to assist in the organization of the Armenian Volunteer Movement. Soon after, he was sent as a fieldworker to the border region of Pasen (between Erzurum and Sarikamish). In 1916, he worked in Moush and Sasoun as a leader and military adviser. In January 1919, he returned to Constantinople and Smyrna.

Sassouni went to the Republic of Armenia in June 1919 and was elected a parliament deputy. He also served as governor in the Alexandropol (Giumri) region. Playing a major role in the anti-Bolshevik rebellion of February 18, 1921, he acted as minister of the interior in the Committee for the Salvation of the Fatherland, which governed Armenia until Soviet forces reoccupied Armenia. After the return of the Communists, Sassouni escaped, eventually settling in Paris.

Sassouni used Paris as a base of operations for about 10 years, until the early 1930s, when he settled in Beirut. During the 1920s and 1930s, he spent considerable time in Eastern Anatolia, working closely with the Kurdish liberation movement on behalf of the ARF. His efforts there earned him wide respect within the Kurdish community.

In Beirut, Sassouni continued to work as a leader of the ARF, becoming a respected elder statesman of the community. He served for many years as a member of the ARF Bureau and was one of the founders of the ARF's *Pakine* literary monthly.

Of his published works, *The Kurdish National Movements and Armeno-Kurdish Relations* (1932, revised 1968) is especially important, as it is considered one of the definitive eyewitness accounts of the Kurdish struggle of the 1920s and 1930s.

He was among a group of ARF leaders who were permitted to visit Soviet Armenia in the 1970s.

Sassouni died in Beirut. He was 88.

*

Even though the prisons of Kharpert, Malatya, and Diyarbekir were full of [Kurdish] prisoners facing the horror of hangings and firing squads, even worse conditions were to be found in the remote regions. Every village or group of villages was subject to this or that regiment or commander, and there the trials were much more speedy and the executions not heard about. Besides all this, the programs of annihilation were being implemented without distinguishing between the innocent and the guilty. In those villages, hundreds, thousands of those arrested would gather in the square, lamenting that only a few dozen of their number would actually be able to have their case heard before the emergency courts.

From "The Kurdish National Party (Hoybun)," Hairenik Monthly, *March 1931*

SOGHOMON TEHLIRIAN
1897–1960

TEHLIRIAN WAS BORN in the village of Nerkin Bagarich, in the Erzurum region, and grew up in nearby Erzincan (Yerznga). He began his education at an Evangelical school in Erzincan, then attended the Ketronakan School of Constantinople. He began his higher education in engineering at a German university but returned to Erzincan when the First World War broke out.

In June 1915, during the deportation of Erzincan Armenians,

Tehlirian witnessed the murder of his mother and brother, along with the rape and murder of his three sisters. He was struck on the head and left for dead. He survived and escaped to Tiflis, where he joined the ARF.

He participated in volunteer units commanded by General Antranig and also took part in the Volunteer regiment commanded by Sebouh.

In 1921 he was assigned to the ARF's Operation Nemesis, which sought to punish Turkish officials guilty of organizing and carrying out the Armenian Genocide.

Tehlirian's main target was Talaat Pasha, one of the triumvirate of Young Turk leaders who had ruled in the last days of the Ottoman Empire; he was a former minister of the interior and a grand vizier (prime minister). Talaat was killed by Tehlirian with a single bullet on the morning of March 15, 1921, in Berlin, in broad daylight. Tehlirian did not flee the scene and was immediately arrested.

He was tried for murder but was exonerated by the German court. His trial became a highly sensational event, examining not only Tehlirian's guilt but also that of Talaat Pasha for the Armenian deportations and mass killings.

The trial influenced Polish lawyer Raphael Lemkin, who was later to coin the term "genocide." He reflected on the trial, "Why is a man punished when he kills another man? Why is the killing of a million a lesser crime than the killing of a single individual?"

After the assassination, Tehlirian moved to Serbia and married Anahit Tatikian, who was also from Erzincan. The couple moved to Belgium and lived there until 1945, when they moved to San Francisco.

Tehlirian died in 1960 and is buried at the Ararat Cemetery in Fresno, California.

*

This is how Tehlirian himself describes that moment forever ingrained in Armenian history, the assassination of Talaat:

I awoke in the morning earlier than usual; the sun's rays had already reached the window of the building across the street. I had just finished my tea and wanted to move the armchair to the window when suddenly I saw Talaat on the balcony of the building. I froze. Was it him? Yes.... He moved forward a step or two, carefully examined the sidewalk, first up, then down, and hung his head, who knows under the weight of what sort of thoughts. Apparently, his life wasn't tranquil after the boundless crime he had committed. In any event, even though five or six years had passed, fear was ever-present for him. He bore on his wide shoulders two public death sentences: The Constantinople War Tribunal's and the Armenian Revolutionary Federation's. The first probably held moral significance for him: Instead of commending him for his great "patriotic" work, in his own land his fellow countrymen had condemned him to death as a common criminal. But time could resolve that "misunderstanding," and future generations would understand the value of his work, if… if only there weren't the death sentence of the Dashnaktsoutiun. All the same, he had been unable to eradicate all the leaders of that party. But who had remained from among his acquaintances? One person, for a fact: Garegin Pastermajian. Did he, I wonder, remember that last conversation with him…? Like a lever he lifted his thick arm, rubbed his forehead with his hand, and went in. I looked at my watch; it was 10 o'clock, his usual time for going to Uhland. I placed my weapon on me, ready to go out.

Suddenly, he appeared by the door and began to descend, heavily, like an elephant. When I got outside onto the street, he was already heading toward Uhland on the opposite sidewalk. Cool-headed judgment was telling me that he wouldn't be able to get away this time, but emotion was stirring up a tempest in me, telling me in multiple tongues, "Run, get to him, cross to the other sidewalk, and diagonally, from behind, at his back, his head, hurry, cross the street…" I stepped off the sidewalk to get behind him, but suddenly something drove me back. The thing that had clearly been confirmed a thousand times seemed, at that moment, suspect: Was it truly him…? "Get across from him, confront him, face to face, hurry, hurry, hurry, run!" I matched his position on the opposite sidewalk and with hurried steps passed him, moving far ahead; I crossed over to the same sidewalk he was on and reversed direction. We were nearing each other. He was moving as if on a stroll, carelessly swinging his walking stick. When only a short distance separated us, a surprising tranquility came over my entire being. As we were about to meet, he looked directly at me; the shudder of death flickered in his eyes. His last step stopped short; he turned slightly to flee, but in a single motion I pulled out my gun and fired a shot at his head…. Talaat seemed to stiffen from the blow, and his powerful body for a second became rigidly tall, unsteady, then like the sawed off trunk of an oak fell with a thud, face forward…. I never could have imagined that the monster would be laid low so easily. For a moment I had the urge to empty all my bullets into his torso, but instead of firing I threw away my handgun. The thick, black blood immediately pooled around Talaat's head, as if oil were spilling forth from a broken pot…. I was enveloped by an internal satisfaction of spirit the likes of which I'd never experienced before. The constant nightmare that had perpetually settled on me, heavy like lead, seemed suddenly to have lifted. Everything had changed, it seemed; my fettered soul was soaring, free, far and wide; as if liberated from a state of being, my thoughts were circulating in all the known corners of the world.

From "Soghomon Tehliran: Recollections," Vahan Minakhorian, Houssaper, *Cairo, 1956*

ARSHAVIR SHIRAGIAN
1900–1973

A RSHAVIR SHIRAGIAN WAS born in Constantinople and grew up around ARF members. As a teen, during the Armenian Genocide, Shiragian was entrusted with delivering messages and transporting weapons for the party.

Shiragian was recruited to take part in the ARF's Operation Nemesis, which sought to punish Turkish officials guilty of organizing and carrying out the Armenian Genocide.

His first target was the traitor Vahe Ishan (Yesayan). According to Shiragian's memoirs, Ishan was "a traitor who was despised by his countrymen, his relatives, and eventually by his own children" and "helped to draw up the list of prominent Armenians who were arrested and deported in 1915." Shiragian assassinated Ihsan on March 27, 1920 in Constantinople.

Shiragian was assigned the task of assassinating Sait Halim Pasha (Grand Vizier of the Ottoman Empire from 1913 to 1917), who was in exile in Rome. On December 5, 1921, Shiragian assassinated him in a taxi. Along with Aram Yerganian, Shiragian was then given the task assassinating both Jemal Azmi, governor of Trebizond during the Genocide, and Behaeddin Shakir, a founding member of the Committee of Union and Progress (Ittihad), both of whom were in Berlin.

On April 17, 1922, Shiragian and Yerganian confronted Azmi and Shakir, who were out walking with their families. Shiragian killed Azmi and wounded Shakir. Yerganian then ran after Shakir and shot him dead.

Shiragian eventually married, and he and his wife, Gaiane, moved to New York in 1923, where they had a daughter, Sonia. He was active in public life and the Armenian community in the New York/New Jersey area.

In 1965, Shiragian published his memoirs, Կտակն էր նահատակներուն (It Was the Legacy of the Martyrs). The memoirs were published in English as *The Legacy: Memoirs of an Armenian Patriot,* in 1976, translated by Sonia Shiragian, and published by the Hairenik Press.

Shiragian died in 1973, in New Jersey. He was 73.

*

Even after so many years, whenever I recall those days, I live through the terror that spread like a disease through Constantinople during the war. At the beginning, thousands of Armenian young men entered the army, responding to the call. Other families sold whatever they could in order to pay the military *bedel* (exemption fee). After collecting millions of dollars, the authorities of the Ittihad government ignored the *bedel* law, gathered the ones who had paid, as well as the ones who had joined the army, and sent them to the war front or organized them into labor battalions. Many of these men died in the filth and disease that plagued the Turkish Army. But many more were murdered by their own Turkish officers. About 120,000 Armenians were massacred after being placed in the so-called labor battalions. Thousands deserted, and thousands of others made their way back to Constantinople, bringing with them horrible stories of systematic murder and torture. So they became fugitives, hiding from the police....

Always expecting the worst, we had come to realize that the Turk could not be trusted. And yet, today, I can admit that very few Armenians, if any, were prepared for the events that started on April 24, 1915. That day, as soon as darkness fell, 250 prominent Armenians—writers, editors, educators, lawyers, Dashnak leaders—were seized in their homes, taken to jail, and eventually sent to Anatolia where they were massacred as a prelude to the slaughter of one and a half million other Armenians. The seizures began around 8 PM as groups of police officers carrying lanterns closed in on the Armenian neighborhoods. Men who had retired for the night were told that they would be brought back within the hour and that there was no need even to change their clothes.... The men were taken at first to local police stations.... They were moved from place to place, deeper and deeper into the labyrinth of Turkish political jails. By the week's end, they had already been sent into the interior of Turkey....

Within the next few days, many more prominent leaders were arrested. When Krikor Zohrab and Vartges Serengiulian, two Armenian members of the Turkish Parliament, appeared before the Grand Vizier, Premier Sait Halim Pasha, to lodge a formal protest, they were given evasive answers.... They were deported and killed.... Within a few months about 2,500 men, the top leadership of the Armenians, had been taken forever from our midst.

During the same evening, April 24, that our nation was being decapitated, another terrible event took place which has been virtually unrecorded. Thousands of young Armenian provincials who had come to Constantinople to work as laborers—*hamals*, doorkeepers, messengers—were jailed and eventually deported and killed. These poor young Armenians had left their families behind in their villages. Some of them had walked hundreds of miles to get to the big city. In Constantinople, they willingly did the most menial and hardest of jobs, working a 13-hour day for the equivalent of ten dollars a month. Most of this money was sent back to their wives to buy food for their children, to their parents to buy seeds or a new farm animal.... But they were young and strong and incorruptibly Armenian and Christian, and the Turks regarded them as a threat to Turkish rule. It was easy for the Turkish police to round up these 5000 men in one night and hustle them off to jail and death. On April 25, not one of these men was at his usual station in the city and not one of these men ever came back....

During those terrible war years, the Armenians of Constantinople had a noble attitude toward their endangered compatriots. They made heroic efforts to turn their homes into hiding places, sharing the bread of their mouths with those unfortunate, persecuted people. Without complaint, they subjected themselves to danger, daily crises, financial difficulties, humiliating and terrifying police searches. In those days of terror, the despised became the virtuous; the drunks, the prostitutes, the ruffians—all the usual customers of police stations throughout the world—helped to find and distribute bread and food. And they were always loyal and discreet. The upper-class, conservative landlords, who for years had turned their backs on revolutionary movements, gave shelter to the fugitive, as did the *Esnaf*—the middle class—who had been the main nerve in all fields of Armenian life. How is it possible to forget the touching behavior of Armenian grandmothers and of old maids… who had led sheltered, orderly lives for so long within their family circles and who now, with wonderful dedication, shared their 250 grams of daily bread ration with the fugitives and even acted as laundresses and chambermaids, washing clothes, and changing bedding. The police announcements and threats were powerless against that resistance movement. It seemed as if everyone had vowed to save as many lives as possible.

From The Legacy: Memoirs of an Armenian Patriot, *Hairenik Press, 1976*

www.ingramcontent.com/pod-product-compliance
Lightning Source LLC
Chambersburg PA
CBHW031321160426
43196CB00007B/606